P.U.S.H.

Persist Until Success Happens

Featuring
Ashley L. Burton

P.U.S.H.

**Persist Until
Success Happens**
Featuring
Ashley L. Burton

Powerful and Insightful Lessons
on Success and Persistence

Ashley L. Burton

Johnny Wimbrey

Matt Morris

Sashin Govender

and other top influencers

WIMBREY TRAINING SYSTEMS
SOUTHLAKE, TEXAS

Published by Wimbrey Training Systems
550 Reserve Street, Suite 190
Southlake, Texas 76092

Printed in the United States of America

ISBN: 978-1-951502-29-4

Table of Contents

Foreword

Les Brown

P.U.S.H. is a shining example of *it doesn't matter where you start out; what really matters is where you're going.* That all-important concept prevents you from allowing your circumstances to determine your reality.

The life experiences of the P.U.S.H. authors have proven you can make incredible things happen in your life, if you are willing to do whatever is required and take the initiative to pursue your dreams. They have accomplished many tremendous things in their lives, and they generously share what they have learned along the way. If you go step-by-step through their proven methods, you will transform your life and experience the health, wealth, and happiness we all hope for. You have all the power you need to transform your life already inside you, and P.U.S.H. will show you how to tap into it.

Each inspiring and enlightening chapter will elevate your life beyond your current circumstances and strengthen your life's mission. Your unique mission, coupled with a strong belief in yourself and in the power of reinventing your life and transforming who you are at this minute into who you can become, will create the potential for remarkable and unlimited achievement in your life.

When you finally know and understand who you were truly made to be, you can begin to tap into the innate power of your own uniqueness. That power will provide you with freedom and life will no longer hold you back. What you've done or not done in your life to this point will no longer matter. You will have the positive energy to move forward without regard to your past.

Although you cannot relive the past, you can learn much about yourself as a result of having lived it. This self-analytic process requires a lot of honesty with yourself as well as the willingness to do whatever it takes to reach your destiny. Of *all* the skills, knowledge, and experience you acquire in this life, the single most valuable is knowledge of the role you are to play on this earth for the sake of your destiny.

P.U.S.H. is designed to empower you with the secret process of success used by those who not only talk the talk, but more importantly, walk the walk. Read it with an open heart and *P.U.S.H.!*

CHAPTER ONE

Pushing Toward Greatness

Johnny Wimbrey

There's never been a millionaire named *Wimbrey* before. I am the first. I did not come from wealth; my father was a garbage man. Nobody ever worked harder than my dad, but he was by no means a millionaire. I don't know anyone on either side of my family—black or white—who had anywhere close to a million dollars in the bank when they died.

Growing up, I never expected an inheritance or imagined getting access to a trust fund when I turned eighteen. Nothing like that existed for me. But it will exist for my children, because the chapter you are about to read was written by a genuine, self-made, first-generation millionaire.

Let's take a step back from the money.

Instead, I want to talk about your character. Becoming successful—becoming that first-generation millionaire—has *everything* to do with the character you bring to the table. Before you can even start thinking about the money, the success, the clout, first you must—*must*—have a conversation with your character, your true character, the person you are when no one is watching.

Without the right character in place—without knowing who you are and what you are capable of—you will never achieve and maintain success.

That's what this book is about. *P.U.S.H.* is not about closing sales, or how to run a multimillion-dollar company, or how to cash in on your side hustle so you can quit your day job. This book is about building the character you need in order to succeed.

Do the work. Lock it up. Make it happen for yourself and your family. Everything you do from now on is in your control.

Every millionaire I've trained, coached, or mentored, was broke and hungry when I met them. They are multimillionaires today, not because of their business acumen or their ability to convince the people they meet to buy something. No. It's because I have ingrained in them the three essential pillars they need to have the character of a first-generation millionaire. If you don't build and exercise these pillars, success will be miniscule and fleeting.

Before you start flipping through this book, ask yourself if you have the desire to disrupt the past to create a new you. There are no shortcuts here. There is no cheating. You must do the work.

Do you have the drive to transform yourself into a person who knows for a fact that you will not die working?

That you will not leave debt to your children and your children's children?

That your family members will be able to live off your work; that *they* will not die working?

Are you ready to be the person in your family who finally stops that cycle?

If so, you must be ready to learn about yourself, to allow yourself to discover things that you thought you had forgotten or hidden away, to transform into someone who has the character of a first-generation millionaire. If you are truly ready to make this change, then read on.

The three pillars essential to the character of every first-generation millionaire I know are:

VALUE: Do you value yourself and your abilities? If you truly want to succeed in life with a solid foundation, first you need to understand your value.

FAITH: Do you have faith in yourself? Not in your ideas. Not in your team. Not in your product. Not in your website. Not even in your family. In *yourself.*

When things go south, when your best employees quit, or when your product gets trumped in the marketplace, do you have faith that you will be able to start from scratch and create success all over again? You must have faith in yourself and your abilities. Otherwise, the very first wave will wash you away completely.

COMMITMENT: Do you have the commitment to take this all the way? Are you honest enough with yourself to ensure that you will give this effort 100 percent of your energy 100 percent of the time? Without commitment, quitting is too easy. Without commitment, you will never be a first-generation millionaire.

Think of wealth-mastery as a house you plan to renovate. You can change the doors, redo the windows, and add a garage, yet there are some walls that your contractor will tell you that you cannot touch. Those walls are integral to the structure of the house. Without them, everything will start to crumble.

These three pillars—value, faith, and commitment—are like those load-bearing walls. You can't get rid of them, you can't negotiate with them, and you can't succeed without them.

Let's talk about **value**. When I was twenty-five years old, I was asked to speak at a well-known church. I wasn't asked to speak to leadership or the congregation but to the leaders' children, the youth of the church. Now, I am always nervous talking to children, but I am especially nervous when it's the children of the leaders we all respect. They're exposed to phenomenal teachings every day. They are constantly surrounded by greatness. It is in their blood. I had to improve on what they already knew, so the topic I chose that day was something all children should hear about starting from a young age. I spoke to them about their value.

I pulled out a $100 bill and showed it to the group. I asked, "How much is this worth?" The children laughed and told me it was worth $100.

Then I folded it in half and asked them again, "How much is *this* worth?" Again, they answered that it was still worth $100.

I asked, "Why doesn't the value change when I folded the bill?"

The children answered with confidence, "Even folded, it is still worth $100."

"What if I fold it again?" I asked as I folded the bill. Now it was a quarter of its original size, yet the children were sure it was still worth $100.

As though I was unconvinced, I said, "You're telling me that if I decrease the size and visibility to a *quarter* of what it was, that the value is still there?"

The group looked at me like I was crazy.

"*Yes!*" they all screamed.

"What if I fold it *again*? What if I crumple it up and throw it on the ground? What if it gets muddy and it looks like garbage? What if I step on it? Then what is it worth?"

"Brother Johnny," they shouted back, "it's *still* worth $100!"

"So, you're telling me that as long as it stays intact—as long as I can smooth it out, rinse it off, make it straight—there is nothing I can do to this piece of paper to cause it to lose its value?"

They all nodded back at me.

I looked at them. "What would you do if someone stepped on your dreams? Crumpled up your ambitions and aspirations? Folded you in half? Mentally, emotionally? Would you lose your value?"

Silence.

Then I asked, "How can this man-made object, this bill made of paper, have more value than you, a God-made object?"

You *must* value yourself if you want to be a first-generation millionaire. It is one of the core characteristics you need to succeed on this journey. If someone tries to fold you in half, crumple you up, or step on you—*and they will*—you must know that nothing and nobody can take away your value. Knowing this as a certainty and exercising this value is something I learned at a young age.

This book will show you how to internalize that feeling and use it to empower yourself as you work to make your first million dollars.

The second pillar is **faith**. I'm not talking about your faith in God; I'm talking about your faith in *yourself*.

Where is that faith in yourself? In *your* abilities? In *your* drive? Before you answer these questions, think about the last chair you sat in; perhaps the one you are sitting in right now. When you were ready to sit down, you didn't check out the chair before you sat. You simply walked up to it and sat. When you go to a restaurant or to see a play, you don't inspect the chair in which you are about to sit. You just sit. You have faith that the chair will do what it was designed to do and hold you.

Now, do you have that same faith in yourself? Or do you say to yourself, "What if I call this person, and they say no? It's going to hurt my feelings." Or, "What if my employees don't think I know what I am doing?"

You didn't talk to *the chair* about being there for you, about doing its job, about not letting you down. But when you must do the thing that needs to be done, do you start asking yourself if it's even possible? If so, *why?* Why do you have more faith in the chair than you do in your own ability to be a first-generation millionaire?

You *must* have faith in yourself or you will never succeed. It's a fact that I have proven over and over again.

When I was presented with an opportunity to expand my team, I flew to South Africa, Australia, and London—all on my own dime. My company didn't want to send me. They didn't want to take the risk; they didn't want to invest in something that was not a sure thing.

But I had faith in myself. I knew if I traveled to those places, I could build the relationships, build the partnerships, and create something out of nothing. I had faith that the very same executives who stayed behind would soon see what I was capable of achieving and follow me across continents.

I want you to have that same faith in yourself. Take your faith that a man-made chair will hold you up and apply that faith to you, a *God-made* person. Only when you are able to do this will you have what it takes to be a first-generation millionaire.

Alongside **value** and **faith**, there is **commitment**. When I say "commitment," I mean being *your* definition of amazing, not someone else's. You *know* what you are masterful at—everyone is masterful at something. But when you are blessed and gifted in a certain area, it's so easy to hide behind someone else's definition of greatness, even if you know better.

Just because someone says you are the best salesperson, promoter, or marketing mind they have ever seen, that doesn't mean that it is *your* best. I am at the top of my field. I speak in front of thousands of people. I make millions each year. But that is still not *my* best. I am writing this book because I want to commit to what I am called to do. I could easily sit back on my earnings and retire before I turn fifty-five.

But that is not the mindset of a first-generation millionaire.

And that is not the mindset I want for you.

To understand your commitment to your goal, imagine a vending machine. If you want some chips but you only feel like eating half the bag, you still have to put in the whole dollar. The machine will never give you half the chips for 50 cents. If you put in 50 cents, the machine will give you *nothing*. You need to commit to the whole bag. You need to put in that whole dollar. There is no negotiation.

You may *say* you want to be a first-generation millionaire but then try to negotiate your life away. You don't commit to waking up two hours early to chase leads and do research. You don't stay at work late to follow up on calls and ideas. You just want to put in that fifty cents and get that half bag of chips.

Stop that behavior *now*!

Before you read any further, you *must* commit to the

whole bag. You simply cannot negotiate commitment to your goal if you want to be a first-generation millionaire.

There's nothing wrong with negotiating; it's a valuable skill to have. but *never* negotiate your commitment to this journey. You will not become a first-generation millionaire without committing to it 100 percent.

If you know that you cannot give everything you have to these three pillars—*value, faith*, and *commitment*—stop reading now. These pillars are the foundation of your character, which will not only bring you that success but allow you to *keep it*. Your character, that will pick you up when you fall. Your character, that you will pass along to your children so they can continue along this path.

If you are obsessed with the numbers on your bank statement, your rank in a company, or the amount of sales you close without being equally obsessed with the quality of your character, you will fail. I can give you all the information you need on how to close a sale, pitch to investors, or run a business, but it won't mean *anything* unless you invest in your character first.

P.U.S.H. is your first step toward investing in your own character. These three pillars will carry you on this journey to being a first-generation millionaire.

Remember the $100 bill that keeps its value, no matter what's done to it.

Remember the man-made chair in which you have so much faith.

Remember the vending machine that demands you go all in or get nothing.

If you truly want to have this, to build this, to be a first-generation millionaire, you must value what you bring to the table. You need to have faith in yourself. And you must commit to your cause.

This book is not for everyone. *P.U.S.H.* is for those of you who are willing to change the trajectory of your lives. It is for you who are ready to change who you are in order to take the next step, for you who are willing to do the work, and for you who are determined to own the person you will become.

This book is your roadmap to greatness. Do the work. Lock it up. Make it happen for yourself and your family. Everything you do from now on is in your control. Don't let anyone tell you otherwise.

With these pillars and the lessons from the journey we are about to embark on together, success is right in front of you. Build and maintain your true character—who you are when it is just you and yourself.

Laying this foundation is your first step to being a first-generation millionaire. Let's get started.

P.U.S.H.

Biography

Johnny Wimbrey is a speaker, author, trainer, and motivator, working with sales teams, high-profile athletes, politicians, and personalities around the world.

Johnny Wimbrey

He has launched three companies (Wimbrey Training Systems, Wimbrey Global, and Royal Success Club International) and heads a sales team of thousands in more than 50 countries, overseeing an active customer database of half a million families.

Johnny shares his powerful message through speaking engagements around the world. He also has a wide media following and has appeared as a guest expert and panelist on television shows including the *Steve Harvey Show, Judge Faith, E! News,* and *The Today Show.*

Johnny's first book, *From the Hood to Doing Good*, has almost 250,000 copies in print or digital editions.

He has collaborated on several other books including *Conversations of Success, Multiple Streams of Determination,* and *Break Through*; more than 600,000 copies of his books are in print.

Johnny and his wife, Crystal, are parents of two daughters and a son. They have co-founded a nonprofit, Wimbrey WorldWide Ministries, which has built six schools in Central America and helped fund water purification systems in Africa.

Contact Information

Johnny D. Wimbrey

Master Motivation/Success Trainer

Most Requested Topics:
Motivation/Keynote
Overcoming Adversity
Youth Enrichment
Leadership/Sales
www.johnnywimbrey.com

 @Wimbrey

@Wimbrey

 Wimbrey

 JohnnyWimbrey

 Wimbrey

 Wimbrey

CHAPTER TWO

Building and Following the Pyramid of Success

John M. Santiago, Jr.

My parents, Salud and John M. Santiago, Sr., immigrated from the Philippines, my dad during the 1920s and my mom 30 years later. They worked hard as a midwife/homemaker and a pantry chef, raising four children in a two-bedroom house. My dad believed in education, and he often said to us, "Work hard; get a good education so you can get a good job."

We listened. My first two years of college were spent at Los Angeles City College, and to supplement my scholarship, I worked at McDonald's, picking up trash in the parking lot, cooking hamburgers, frying fries, washing cooking utensils, and sweeping and mopping floors. Eventually I became a swing manager and started to pick up some leadership and training skills, and even trained new McDonald's franchisees.

I spent my very limited free time either playing basketball with my McDonald's buddies after we closed the store or watching UCLA basketball on TV. In those years, UCLA basketball was incredibly exciting to watch; Coach John Wooden's unmatched streak of 10 national championships in 12 years was still alive.

The Pyramid of Success can be the character framework for anyone who wants to pursue their passion

---

It was tough going when I transferred to UCLA; I took an Air Force ROTC scholarship to pay my way and I was barely coping. Keeping up with demanding engineering and ROTC program requirements meant burning a lot of midnight oil, and my friends placed bets on how quickly I'd fall asleep during lectures.

THE PYRAMID OF SUCCESS

UCLA gave me more than just the technical skill set of an engineer. As a knowledgeable basketball fan, I watched in amazement how poised and confident Wooden's players remained throughout the game and how his key players would step up when needed. The coach won with tall players and he won with short players. He won with talented teams and he won with less talented teams. He worked with what he had. I decided I'd do my best to copy Wooden's mindset for success.

During the post-game winner's interviews, Wooden talked more about supporting the team than about the star players. I still admire how he smoothly applied his team philosophy of *We supersedes Me.* His championship record, in my humble opinion, will never be broken.

When I read Wooden's biography, I was in awe of his meticulous player preparation during practice sessions. What's amazing is that he never mentioned the word *Winning*; instead he emphasized *Doing Your Best.*

Why was John Wooden successful as a coach and mentor?

Wooden spent years developing the *Pyramid of Success.* He wanted to teach his players about being successful in life, and he used basketball as the means to educate them. I too attempted to follow his *Pyramid of Success,* his gift to the world, during my 40-plus years as a military officer and a university professor.

Wooden's *Pyramid* and his many books all focus on continuous self-development and improvement, getting out of your comfort zone and being the best that you are capable of being, and living up to your potential by using your God-given talents. He urged us to fix our weaknesses and improve ourselves as well as improve the team by helping to improve each individual.

For example, I wasn't taught at home or at school about investment and starting my own business, so I made a point to learn all I could (and became successful at it). I also purposefully became a voracious reader.

This chapter isn't long enough to fully describe the nuggets of wisdom in Wooden's *Pyramid of Success* and how they relate to leadership. The *Pyramid's* cornerstones are enthusiasm and industriousness, and they can be summarized as *Love What You Do.*

Part of your real-life journey is finding your passion and your purpose, and they're not always easy to find. For help, Google Wooden's *Pyramid of Success* and take advantage of the free download offered on his site. His book, *On Leadership,* isn't free, but it's worthwhile ordering.

The *Pyramid of Success* can be the character framework for anyone who wants to pursue their passion, and it makes a great gift, especially when customized. I have given copies as graduation gifts with the graduate's name on top and their photo printed on the *Pyramid.*

Wooden was a leader who created future leaders, and he designed the *Pyramid* to build leaders. As a coach and mentor, he ensured his players had a high graduation rate, and many of them contributed to society as authors, ministers, doctors, teachers, coaches, television broadcasters, and many other worthwhile fields.

After graduating and being commissioned as an officer, I served in the U.S. Air Force for the next 26 years, specializing in engineering, research, and development of systems to protect us and our freedoms. Five years after graduation, I married my lovely wife Emily on Valentine's Day. Our marriage was one of the best decisions I've made in my life, and we're still happily married 37 years later.

During my entire Air Force career, I attempted to follow the leadership values of the *Pyramid of Success,* and I acted upon its values. I felt honored when I was given a plaque picturing the *Pyramid of Success* with my name on top as a going-away gift. In my next assignment, I used the *Pyramid* as a pass-along-award to recognize a worthy individual, with the proviso that it be passed to another recipient on a quarterly basis.

An engraved metal copy of the *Pyramid* was presented to me at my retirement ceremony, and it's proudly hung in a shadow box on my home office bragging wall.

BUILDING MY OWN PYRAMID

I loved all my military assignments and learned as many technologies as I could while getting leadership experience. One of my best assignments was as a professor of electrical engineering at the U.S. Air Force Academy. I taught there for 4.5 years while completing my own Ph.D. Though it was tough, my colleagues looked after me and I had a great supervisor. For one entire semester, colleagues taught my classes while I focused on writing and defending my dissertation. My supervisor even made sure I checked off items on the list to compete for promotion to major.

My best assignment was to the European Office of Aerospace Research and Development in London. My blanket orders allowed me to travel anytime and anywhere in Europe, the former Soviet Union, Middle East, and Africa, as well as to laboratories in the United States. My job was "to keep those engineers and scientists from the countries of the former Soviet Union busy so they won't go to the bad guys."

As Deputy Commander and Chief Scientist, my mission was like a dating service, matching the talented foreign engineering/scientists with the needs of the military engineers/scientists. I viewed my position as a scientific ambassador, interacting with top scientists and engineers at several conferences and workshops.

In July 2003, I retired from the U.S. Air Force with 26 years of service, and then decompressed for about 15 months, catching up with family and friends while figuring out my next venture. I also spent time learning to build websites and use internet marketing technologies to deliver online math, science, and engineering courses.

A former Air Force colleague who was the Dean/Chair of Engineering at Colorado Technical University (CTU) found out what I was doing, and he invited me for an interview as an adjunct professor. When I discovered how much work four new courses required, I asked for a full-time position and got it.

During the next 14 years as a professor of electrical and systems engineering at CTU, I taught more than 40 courses in math, physics, and engineering, including 12 graduate courses. I authored more than 50 published papers and one book, *Circuit Analysis for Dummies* (CAFD). I would have preferred the title, *Circuit Analysis for Newbies*, but then again, I may start a multimedia eBook series with that name. My book was the result of a literary agent discovering the hundreds of videos that I'd posted on YouTube.

ENGINEERING A NATION

A major highlight of my years as professor was during Engineering Week in February 2018. My colleagues and I created four hour-long product knowledge training sessions for admissions staff and success coaches at CTU on various engineering disciplines. I titled the sessions *What Engineering Is All About,* and our goal was to increase engineering enrollment.

The sessions received high ratings and positive feedback, and within a few months, engineering enrollment increased 20%.

Here are some of my favorite engineering nuggets:

Theodore von Kármán, an aerospace engineer and scientist, wrote, "Scientists discover the world that exists; engineers create the world that never was."

The Founding Fathers were really engineers because they engineered and created a government that never had been imagined before. They put together the 28 principles of freedom, for the first time in history, including separation of powers, checks and balances, and natural law.

The exceptional and collective genius of the Founding Fathers resulted in a 5,000-year leap in history when compared to the previous 5,000 years. The collection of these 28 principles resulted in a climate of free market economics, yielding an explosion of inventions and technical discoveries in merely 250 years.

George Washington was another role model and leader I admired. Few people know that Engineering Week is held during George Washington's birthday. Why? Because he was an accomplished surveyor at age 17 and an agricultural engineer. He engineered tools for wheat processing and invented a new plow that was a combination of plow and seeder. He experimented with new techniques in crop rotation, soil fertilization, and livestock management.

President Washington created the Army Corps of Engineers and he developed the country's first engineering school, which evolved into what's now known as U.S. Military Academy at West Point. To this day, all our military academies have a heavy focus on math, physics, and engineering courses.

Washington was a multi-talented strategic and visionary leader, and that's one of many reasons I admire him. He designed and built Mount Vernon without assistance of an architect. While president, he pushed construction of roads, canals, the Capitol, docks, and ports, as well as other waterways, the physical equivalent of today's internet highway, making connections to create value for society. He pushed new efforts to extract coal and ores. He pushed with purpose to develop manufacturing resources. He also developed a prototype submarine.

Most important, President Washington pushed for passage of the first U.S. Patent Act in 1789, wanting to encourage and protect individuals' creativity by allowing them to have a monopoly on their inventions for a period of time, giving them the chance for their idea to become reality and capitalize on it.

And that, my friends, is why President Washington and the Founding Fathers were great visionary leaders.

The Founding Fathers created a government with a purpose to transform lives that benefits society as a whole. However, a republican constitution cannot survive unless the people and their leaders are moral and virtuous. The *Pyramid of Success* can serve as a great framework, providing criteria to judge and select individuals who are moral and virtuous leaders.

SHAPING THE FUTURE

After serving and retiring from the military and as a university professor, I started on my third venture as a bucket-list entrepreneur in June 2019. My passion is life-long learning and teaching people how to achieve personal freedom and independence. But I also would like to have more fun, fulfillment, and freedom at this stage of my life. My plan is to travel while doing online teaching on topics including engineering, entrepreneurship, leadership, and U.S. history. With today's amazing technologies, communicating your passion worldwide while completing your bucket list is indeed possible.

I believe engineering or entrepreneurship are powerful means of transforming lives and society. Learning engineering is indeed a challenge. Learning and doing entrepreneurship is just as challenging when it comes to personal development. When both engineering and entrepreneurship work in tandem, you are stoppable.

As an engineer, by leveraging your technical skill set and having an entrepreneurial mindset, you will have a fulfilled and meaningful life.

I also want to pursue my passion to create and launch an online preparatory program for military veterans and active-duty service members to prepare them to enter either an engineering or entrepreneurial degree program at a traditional university or college. In this new venture, I would love to show people why it's important to look at the bigger picture and understand why recognizing opportunities, evaluating markets, and learning from mistakes will eventually result in creating value for society. Creating value for others can shape people's future and transform their lives so they can live a life of freedom.

To lay the groundwork for the preparatory program for veterans and military active-duty service members, I'm working with the Kern Entrepreneurial Engineering Network (KEEN), a network of 40-plus universities/colleges to combine the technical skill sets and the entrepreneurial mindsets we believe will help revolutionize the teaching of engineering.

For the engineering preparatory program, we start simply with an introduction to engineering, pre-algebra, algebra, trigonometry, and pre-calculus. Why learn math? Because engineering is essentially applied math, used as a simple tool to see if your ideas are technically feasible and economically viable. Math allows you to think critically while making and relying on your own decisions.

My vision is to develop a program to educate the public on engineering, entrepreneurship, leadership, and U.S. history. My dream is to customize this venture and have it accessible and affordable for less fortunate families in the Philippines.

With this dream in my mind, I founded and became CEO of Freedom Institute of Technology (FIT). Our motto is *Why FIT in when YOU are born to STAND OUT!* We have a work-in-progress website with introductory presentations using advanced text-to-speech technologies and artificial intelligence for talking avatars. While it's not a full-blown course site yet, it's a glimpse of what we are planning and it will continuously evolve.

I've included my mentor, Coach Wooden, his *Pyramid of Success*, plus vintage videos and testimonials from his players and colleagues. We're working on another website that holistically integrates the entrepreneurial/leadership mindsets.

My goal is to empower families to reach personal and financial freedom while not borrowing money from the government, family, or friends.

I hope to show you what freedom looks like and teach you how to reach it.

You live in this great land of opportunity and freedom that God has provided for us. What's *your* dream?

Biography

As a U.S. Air Force officer and an educator, John M. Santiago, Jr., won many prestigious scientific achievement and teaching excellence and innovation awards, including two at the United States Air Force Academy and three at Colorado Technical University, including the 2015 Educator of the Year for Teaching Innovation.

John M. Santiago, Jr.

His distinguished educational career includes a B.S. (cum laude) from University of California, Los Angeles, an M.S. from the Air Force Institute of Technology, and a Ph.D. from the University of New Mexico, all in Electrical Engineering. He received an additional M.S. degree in National Resource Strategy, from what is now Dwight D. Eisenhower School for National Security and Resource Strategy.

John is the author of *Circuit Analysis for Dummies* and has produced DVDs and video lessons in circuit analysis and design, differential equations, trigonometry, pre-algebra, and introduction to engineering. A sought-after speaker, John specializes in Leadership, Diversity (in thought), and Commitment to Excellence.

John is founder and CEO of Freedom Institute of Technology (FIT), a revolutionary online platform that introduces the public to engineering entrepreneurship, leadership, and financial literacy.

John always manages to find time for his hobbies: billiards, reading, and, of course, playing basketball.

Contact information

Email: john.santiago@e-liteworks.com
Website: http://FreedomInstituteOfTechnology.com
http://FreedomUniversity.TV
http://CircuitAnalysisForDummies.com
http://facebook.com/freedomuniversitytv
http://vipplatinumescapes.worldventures.biz
http://vipplatinumescapes.dreamtrips.com
https://www.youtube.com/user/drjctu
https://www.youtube.com/user/drjcircuits

CHAPTER THREE

God is Trying to Tell You Something

Toni L. Pennington

I was standing in my kitchen preparing my breakfast when the word *perseverance* flashed in my brain. I thought, "Stop right now and go write that down!" My mind runs faster than my hand writes, so I picked up the phone to make a voice note. There was a message from my friend Kim, whom I'd thought of just thirty minutes earlier.

"The sermon I heard in church this morning made me think of you. Watch it online." Kim shared some highlights, and they were identical to thoughts I just had. It was as though I had been in church with her.

When I went to my laptop to write, the screen opened to YouTube and I saw the words, *God Is Trying to Tell You Something*.

The morning's intertwined events reminded me that my experiences and life lessons are not only for me. I need to share them and help others step into the lives they should be living, their *best* lives.

Do you wonder what this has to do with perseverance? I'm glad you asked.

Perseverance doesn't appear out of nowhere. It's within you. It's within us all when we want something badly enough. Sadly, we don't always recognize it right away. Sometimes we miss it because circumstances (or people) beat us down and we make the mistake of listening to the negative words that are sent our way. Instead, we must say, "*I can do this!* This *is* for me and I'm going to move come hell or high water to get it."

To anyone who is reading this, I want to encourage you to always keep your eye on your prize, no matter what it is.

In addition to my story, I will share the journeys of two students whom I mentored and tutored. They've become friends and colleagues, and I admire them tremendously.

Neslie Lopez

Neslie had no intention of attending college. She joined the Air Force Junior Reserve Officers' Training Corps (ROTC) program at her inner-city high school and believed her career would be in the military. Her parents disagreed, and because she was only 17, she couldn't sign up without their permission. As a star athlete in track and field, she caught the interest of a West Point Military Academy scout, but she didn't have top-tier SAT test scores nor contacts needed for a political nomination.

That year, Neslie met Mary, a classmate who had a diagnosis of Stage II pancreatic cancer. The girls developed a strong friendship, and despite Mary's bad prognosis, they began to plan their college careers. While Mary was in a hospital bed, Neslie studied at a local medical school through a special honors program, but still didn't feel she was smart enough to be a doctor. She thought she'd settle on a more attainable medical career like nursing.

What I do regret is that I didn't pour my whole self into my work.

Neslie was accepted at New Jersey City University and entered the Army ROTC Program at Seton Hall to work toward becoming a second lieutenant. When Mary passed away at just 19, Neslie realized time was finite and regained her courage to chase her passion for medicine.

Her transition to pre-med study was not easy. I met her when she came to my office for tutoring as she struggled with an English term paper. Neslie persisted with her ROTC training; she had the "Can Do, Never Quit" mindset instilled in her by the military.

She excelled in her required English classes and soared in science and mathematics. The next year she paid her knowledge forward and came back to the tutoring center as a science tutor. Today she is a college graduate working at an oncology/hematology practice en route to medical school. She never stopped reaching for the goal that would fulfill the promise and the dream that she and Mary shared.

Jeffrey Aizprua

My friend Jeff immigrated to the United States from Ecuador during an economic crisis, hoping to find ways to help his family back home. The crisis hit during his first year of college in Ecuador while he was studying computer engineering. That career wasn't his dream; he was following his uncle's advice, believing he'd make a substantial amount of money and be a blessing to his family.

When he landed in Florida, Jeff didn't speak any English. He played in a band and worked a variety of odd jobs, though he knew he had more to contribute to the world and desired to help others.

Jeff decided to go back to school, and he moved north to New Jersey and applied to the school where we work together today. The dean of his college major rejected him; he told Jeff to enroll in a community college, get an A, and prove that he deserved to be enrolled in this school. Up for the challenge, Jeff enrolled in the community college. Still struggling with his English, he found himself in two very difficult courses, *Principles of Macroeconomics* and *Introduction to Business*. Within a few weeks, he got a C on his first exam. That's when he got laser focused.

Anticipating the next test would be much more difficult, he used up every minute of his vacation and sick time to study. "Never in my life had I studied so hard.

I didn't understand the words, so I had to memorize everything." His classmates were dumbfounded when the guy who barely spoke English annihilated the test with an A. When he passed the class with a B+, he said to himself, "Okay, maybe I can really do this."

When Jeff landed a solid job as a trucking company dispatcher, he quickly saw the bad behavior rampant in the company and knew he shouldn't stay there very long, but he needed the income. His superiors made his life miserable, even purposely scheduling mandatory meetings when they knew he had class. Jeff didn't care. He had a plan and a goal. "My objective was always to study."

It worked; Jeff was awarded his B.S. with a 3.7 GPA, co-majoring in math and economics with a minor in international studies. But he wasn't done.

Once he was enrolled in his master's program, he was very clear on what he wanted to do. He wanted to study the financial situation in a country that was between the United States and Ecuador economically—China. He went to the president of the university, explained his history and motives, and was awarded a grant for his research.

One month before he was to go on his trip, Jeff was hit by a car. "What do I do?" he thought. "Do I go back and say I can't travel after they've given me $8,000 and the chance of a lifetime, or do I go?"

It was a no-brainer. The trip had taken 18 months to put together and he couldn't pass up the opportunity. So, he flew halfway around the world, in agony during the entire 14-hour flight. His first excursion was walking atop the Great Wall. He did it. Nothing would stop him. "If I had been born a boxer, the referee would have to stop the fight at some point because he would say, 'This guy is never going down!'"

Jeff spent days in classes and conferences at Peking University with students from all over the world who "were fluent in several languages, younger, faster, and smarter," but he pushed through. "I think we all have the power inside us to do whatever we want because we ask for what we want from the Universe." At every turn he met the people he needed to know to advance in his studies and his career, and he made many international friends.

A professor invited Jeff to participate in the National Modern United Nations event. With an international collaboration—a student from South Sudan, an American, and my friend from New Jersey by way of Ecuador—Jeff's Economics Committee won the Outstanding Delegation Award for their presentation.

As he neared completion of his Master's program at Rutgers, another professor suggested that he apply to the American Economics Association program, an elite program that accepts only the top students and prepares them to study economics at the doctoral level. As an English major, I helped edit a paper he presented to his professor, a world-renowned economist, which was a major component of his pre-Ph.D. work.

His new dream was to be admitted into the program that he felt was the best, but something was still nagging at him. While he excelled in economics, he really wanted to focus on environmental issues as they related to economics. The problem was that the director of the program focused on national security, and Jeff didn't believe that he would be considered. By chance (or not), he shared his dilemma with a friend he had made in China.

She said, "What are you talking about? There's a new director and his focus is actually on what you want to study—sustainable development. Go talk to him *now*."

This fall, Jeff will begin his Ph.D. studies in sustainable development and international trade. Throughout his years of struggles and attending classes where language was a major barrier, he always dug deeper, looked forward, and found a way to achieve his goals. I am truly honored to call him my friend.

My Story

My story is not at all like Jeff's or Neslie's—*they* never stopped moving forward. I took time off from school, worked, and let too much time pass before I got back on my path. When I finally focused on continuing my education, I had serious health issues that sidelined entire semesters and knocked me off course.

I wanted to accomplish two major things. First, music. I had wanted to sing from the time I was five years old. As I got older, I simply wanted to do it in front of a huge audience without passing out! (That's another story.) Both the influence, and the inspiration were always there. My household was musical. There was always some type of music playing, from R&B to rock to classical to gospel. The house was never silent. My mother had a beautiful voice and sang all the time. Whenever I was at my grandmother's house, there was music playing, and she would hum as she cooked. Singing was firmly implanted in my brain and soul.

Second, education. Like Jeff, I believe that God puts wants and desires in us and gives us the wherewithal to achieve those things. We just have to act on them. When it was time for me to go to high school, I planned to take tests for several specialized high schools in New York City.

His classmates were dumbfounded when the guy who barely spoke English annihiliated the test with an A.

Of course, my first choice was The High School of Performing Arts, the school made famous by the movie *Fame*. I still remember the heartbreak of that day. I left my middle school in Sheepshead Bay near Coney Island, for my interview at the school. I was supposed to transfer to a different train, but it never came. I still wonder if my directions weren't clear, if it simply wasn't meant to be, or if subconsciously I forced myself to fail without facing my fear of rejection. I was terribly afraid of auditioning and I may have let that fear consume me.

My second choice was Fashion Industries High School in Manhattan. I had become a seamstress when I was 13 and was quite good at it. I made everything I wore except my undergarments! By then, I was very comfortable not looking like everyone else. I took pride in it.

This time I made it to the interview. Of course, I wore a dress I had made myself. Very soon after my interview I received my acceptance letter.

My third choice (actually my father's choice) was Brooklyn Technical High School, a top math and science school. My interest in going there was minimal, but my dad insisted that I try. I passed the test by five points. My fate was sealed. My father didn't care about singing or fashion, he just wanted me to have the best education and future possible.

What I don't regret about that path is that 40 years later the closest true friends I could ever have are the people I met in that school. What I do regret is that I didn't pour my whole self into my work. I made it through most of the way, but ended up leaving in my last semester. I passed all the basic requirements and Regents exams to receive an above-average high school diploma.

That part of my life was done. But I still wanted that fashion education. That never left me. I went to the Fashion Institute of Technology (FIT) and began studying fashion buying and merchandising.

Even though it was a state school and not expensive, I struggled. I wanted to work to earn my own money, but again, I didn't put all my energy into my education. Making money was great, but I spent almost everything I earned. Part-time work became almost full-time whenever I could get the hours. I worked at Macy's flagship store on 34th Street in Manhattan; nine floors of shopping bliss with an employee discount. The temptation was huge for a young person who wasn't financially responsible.

I would take three classes one semester, but only one the next. I wasn't in a rush to finish, but before I knew it four years had passed. Most of my high school friends had finished four-year college degrees, and I hadn't finished a two-year degree. But I kept moving forward. Six years after high school graduation I finally earned my Associates degree. I felt a sense of accomplishment, but a sense of disappointment as well. I wore an internal badge of shame for taking so long to do something I believed I should have conquered much sooner.

Many years would pass before I understood that each person runs their own race. I knew I could earn a four-year degree, but I also really liked making money.

My focus shifted, and I got my dream job as a buyer for chain and independent stores, yet that degree was still nagging at me. Just when I was about to go back to school, I became ill and had my first surgery. The recovery process was slow. It knocked out that semester and kept me from working, so I was eager to get back on my feet and recover my regular income.

Years passed. I continued to get better jobs, making more and more money, yet that elusive degree was always at the back of my mind.

Fast forward fourteen years. I had experienced great musical success, appearing on recordings and singing at Town Hall and Lincoln Center in New York. But still the idea of that degree lingered. I was living in New Jersey by then, and finally in 2004 I enrolled in one class at New Jersey City University. I was disappointed when they only accepted 39 of my 66 credits, but at least I wasn't starting from scratch. The journey toward my coveted B.A. had finally restarted.

At the end of the semester, I was derailed with another surgery. Out of school and with no income, I was anxious to regain my lifestyle and focused on work for a year. Back at school, I finished several semesters before serious new health issues sidelined me. That time I nearly died. I had blood clots in my lungs. In 2007, I faced twelve months from hell, and I spent more nights in the hospital than I ever had in my life.

The next year, sharp clinicians and an unusually high white cell count led to a diagnosis of HIV. This news nearly destroyed me. I wallowed in tears of sadness.

Once again, time passed, but I *knew* I was going to reach my goal. Throughout my setbacks, distractions, and heartaches, I always kept my eye on the prize, one class at a time. In January 2017, I was finally awarded my university diploma with honors, and I couldn't be prouder. I was 54 when I got it done—and I wasn't finished. As this book goes to print, I am halfway through my graduate program.

To anyone who is reading this, I want to encourage you to *always* keep your eye on *your* prize, no matter what it is.

Everyone's prize or goal is not the same and that's okay. I've learned the greatest prize is in the journey. Our best education comes from the trials and lessons we learn along the way. Success comes at the very end and with that success we have something to offer to the ones who will come after us.

Biography

Toni L. Pennington

Toni L. Pennington is a native of Brooklyn, New York, who now lives in Jersey City, N.J. She holds a Bachelor of Arts degree in English from New Jersey City University, where she works as an academic success coach and tutor mentor. She has hosted several student symposiums at the university.

Although she has been a singer for most of her life, she finds great joy in writing. Toni has been published in several issues of *PATHS*, one of the school's literary publications, and co-authored *Break Through featuring Toni L. Pennington* with Les Brown and several well-known international authors. She is currently working on her Master of Arts degree at Southern New Hampshire University.

Contact Information

Email: joyforeverenterprises@gmail.com
Website: joyforeverenterprises.com
Instagram: Joyforever1love

CHAPTER FOUR

Power of Purpose

Fitz P. Mombeleur

Success is going from failure to failure,
without losing your enthusiasm.
—Anonymous

When I was five years old, I believed I could conquer the world. I sat in my front yard in the small town of Carl Junction, Missouri, population *maybe* 3,000. I was watching a parade take place in front of my house, and the faces around me were filled with laughter and joy. The parade overflowed with excitement, happiness, and empowerment. I had never been a part of anything else where people spoke so passionately in what they believed, hoping to make things happen and make a change in their lives. I just loved it there. Just me, my family, and my friends—it was an amazing experience. I was only five, and I was experiencing what I thought was greatness.

When I was seven years old, my dad lost his job and my parents decided to move to New York City. What a change it made in my life, going from a small town with one stoplight and one grocery store, to a major metropolis with seven million people. It was mind-boggling to me. So many people, so many familiar faces—well, so many people who looked like me.

**I didn't know it then, but I surely know it now:
When there is *purpose* for your living,
no one can hold you back.**

I will never forget February—Black History Month—and I was sitting in my brand-new class in Brooklyn with my little cowboy boots on and my little Afro; it was a scary time for me. Interestingly enough, in Missouri we never celebrated Black History Month, so I just thought it was a reason for us to watch a movie in class.

What happened next changed my world view. The teacher started playing the movie *Mississippi Burning,* and I was excited because I hadn't seen it before. Anyone who knows that movie knows it is about the Ku Klux Klan; well, it seemed that everyone knew but me. I started watching it and I was all into the movie—and then it happened, people with white sheets over their heads were parading down the street. That moment my heart sank, I was confused, because in the movie they were portrayed as bad people. In Missouri, when the Ku Klux Klan paraded down the street in front of my house, they were always nice to me. I stood up and said, "That is a lie, they are good people." That didn't go over so well in Brooklyn, New York, and I was sent to the principal's office. I could not understand why. What did I do wrong? I was just seven.

I told the principal that where I came from these people would parade down the street in front of my house all the time; they were passionate speakers and could move a crowd. I always felt like I could conquer the world after hearing one of them speak. I didn't understand why everyone was saying they were bad.

Reality check. I learned that day what the Ku Klux Klan stood for and how they had killed countless African-American people, *my* people. I didn't understand why my life had been spared. My family is Haitian, from the Caribbean, and we're black—as black as they come. They had never touched us.

My family had lived in Missouri for seven years. I was the youngest of four siblings, and we all went to school with these people's kids, played at their houses, and my brother even dated their daughters. What made *us* so much better, what made *us* so different that they left us alone?

Purpose. I didn't know it then, but I surely know it now: When there is purpose for your living, no one can hold you back. You can even have dinner with your enemy and God will protect you so that your enemy doesn't see you for who you are, but instead for who God wants you to be. Purpose can take you from the back of the theater to the stage. Purpose is what keeps you seeing more and more opportunities so you can be the person that God created you to be, the person who will impact the world and impact others.

Purpose; *never* underestimate the power of purpose.

Have you ever wondered why so many things happened in your life that should have destroyed you, but you are still here? Though you are upset, maybe even angry that you are not where you believe that you should be or where you want to be, remember, you aren't dead yet. You are alive, you are moving, you are walking, you are talking, you are constantly preparing for the greatness it seems only you can see. *You have purpose.*

CONTROL YOUR THOUGHTS

When I was that seven-year-old child in a Brooklyn classroom and my young eyes were opened to a reality I never thought humanly possible, at that moment, at that tender age, I had a decision to make. Would I allow the people around me to take my thoughts captive and change what I saw and what I knew? Or would I take control of my thoughts and come up with my own conclusion? See, too many times we allow what is happening around us to dictate how we think, which in turn changes how we respond.

I learned at that very young age that things are not always as they seem, so I began taking hold of my thoughts. Does this mean that I never had a negative thought or that others could not influence me? No, I just learned that *I* held the power in my life. I gave away a lot of that power over the years, and I learned the hard way that we must control our thoughts, we *must* be careful what we allow into our minds.

What we allow into our mind flows out of our mouths. "There is death and life in the tongue." We hear that saying all the time, and we act as if we believe it; however, we do not follow our own advice. Instead, we are constantly speaking and spreading death over our lives; we are constantly spreading doom and destruction whenever we say negative things about ourselves. The odds are that you've said: *I am broke, I will never make it, I am lazy, I am a procrastinator, I will never be rich, I will never work a good job.*

Stop making excuses; stop holding yourself back and get moving. What are you waiting for? Time is *not* on our side.

Even when someone comes along and says to us, "I believe in you!" we're more likely to disagree with them than to agree. We shut them down and say, "No, I'm not worthy, not good enough."

We continue to repeat negativity about ourselves, we believe what we say, and we live a life that lacks purpose. We *must* take control of our thoughts so we can begin to live the purpose that we were created to live.

GET OVER IT!

We have *so* many excuses as to why we are not at the point where we should be in our lives. How many of us have blamed our imperfect childhoods and our imperfect parents for whatever we lack in our lives? We have so many excuses for all we haven't accomplished.

Just stop.

Stop making excuses; stop holding yourself back and get moving. What are you waiting for?

Time is *not* on our side! The one thing we can never get back is our time. The wealthy have the same 24 hours we have each day; it's what they do with their time that makes all the difference. They know their purpose; they know what they need to do in order to accomplish that purpose, and they get it accomplished. Does that mean they don't have obstacles? No. Does that mean they don't have to overcome all the excuses they encounter? No! Does that mean they don't have people in their ear saying they cannot do it? *No*. It's as hard for them as it is for you; they just turn negativity into something positive.

It's time for *you* to channel all your negativity, turn it into positivity, and stop giving other people authority over your life. You don't need anyone's approval to sit here and read this book right now; this tells me that you are destined for greatness. So, I ask you, what are you going to do about it?

Charles Lindbergh said, *"Success is not measured by what a man accomplishes, but by the opposition he has encountered and the courage with which he has maintained the struggle against overwhelming odds."* Are you going to just sit down and wait while you keep making excuses, allowing time to pass you by, or are you going to go, take action, and then make it happen?

What are you waiting for?

INVEST IN YOURSELF

"You need a mentor!" I heard that constantly. "Find someone who's doing what you want to be doing or who has reached where you want to be; ask them to be your mentor so they can help you reach your goals and your dreams." As easy as that sounds, it's not an easy task. These days, it's a bit easier because we have the internet, but in my day, it was much more difficult. Still, that's just an excuse I made for myself, right?

Wrong. I did go out and talk to people on a regular basis, yet no one ever called me back. No one agreed to be my mentor. I thought I was doing something wrong.

When I was a child, I was never a bookworm and didn't enjoy reading, but as an adult I discovered there were books that could help me become a better me. I found books written by people doing the things that *I* wanted to do, and I finally started to read. I assumed this would be a stop-gap measure until I could find a mentor.

I had another issue: I didn't have money to buy the books, and my local library didn't carry this type of book, so I was stuck again, right?

Wrong! Did you know the Barnes & Noble bookstore chain invites you to go inside their stores, pick a book, and read it in the store or coffeeshop without ever having to buy it? Reading in the store meant I had to plan my excursions in advance and make a commitment of time, but it was time *invested*—my time was well spent.

Every day I went to Barnes & Noble for one hour, sat down, and read. My first book was *Rich Dad, Poor Dad,* by Robert Kiyosaki. Yeah, that was a game-changer.

The master teacher Himself gave us the formula in these words: *But the one who endures to the end will be saved.* (Matthew 24:13) So that is just what I did; I stuck with it, day in and day out, sometimes buying a book to read at home.

You don't need anyone's approval to read this book right now. So, I ask you, what are you going to do about it?

Though I never stopped reading, I just didn't get it. President Harry Truman said, "Not all readers are leaders, but all leaders are readers." Yes, fellow readers, it's ironic; we say that all the time, yet so many people still don't read.

At the same time, I continued to search for a mentor, someone who would take the time to see what I saw in myself. When you stick to your plan, you hope that it happens overnight, but that's not true for anyone.

Look at Scot and Eric Martineau and Clate Mask; in a garage in 2001 they founded the software company InfusionSoft (now being branded as Keap). They knew they had the next best thing when it came to technology, and they never gave up on themselves, even when many others did. By 2013, InfusionSoft had raised $125 million in venture capital, of which $54 million was Goldman Sachs' own investment. What if the brothers had quit because no one believed in them? When they were in their garage or the unimposing small storefront that housed their next stage of growth, they had to believe in themselves and never give up. If they had given up, they would not be thriving in their beautiful, modern 90,000-square foot headquarters in Arizona, built around a private football field.

A few years ago when I was talking to God, I asked, "Lord, why is it that I have yet to find anyone to be my mentor? I'm steadily asking, and they're steadily saying 'no,' or 'I don't have time.' Or they say 'Yes,' and then I find myself chasing them down because I'm more of a burden to them than I am a person of interest. God, why can't I find anyone to mentor me?"

In that moment, God responded, *"What do you mean?"*

"Not one person in all these years has taken the time to mentor me," I said.

"You have had some of the best mentors that money could buy," was the reply.

I still didn't understand. "How is that possible? Who and where are these people, as I surely didn't see them?"

The Lord said nothing more, and I went home pondering about what He had shared with me.

When I chose the next book to read, at that moment I understood what He meant. I was so busy looking for the right person, I didn't realize I had many of them sitting in my living room all along. I was being mentored by the best of the best.

In my lifetime, I have probably spent twenty-five thousand dollars on books. I buy books all the time and I have been mentored by Robert Kiyosaki, John C. Maxwell, Bishop T.D. Jakes, Joel Osteen, Max Lucado, Robert Morris, Tom Rath, Napoleon Hill, Dr. C. Thomas Anderson, Bill Winston, Les Brown, Dr. Myles Munroe, and so many more.

God had told me that I didn't find a physical mentor because He understood how I learn. He knew if I had found that one person I was searching for, I would have stopped reading—and learning, and growing—and I would not have invested in myself the way I needed to fulfill the "leaders are readers" promise. I laughed, and at that moment, I realized He loves me so much that He gave me the best of the best at the price even I could afford.

Are you still making excuses as to why you cannot invest in yourself? I *always* bet on me!

Transform your thinking, transform your life

The time is now. Your transformation begins when you change your thoughts and start to speak life into yourself. Our creator has said He has given you the power to create wealth, yet too many of us are passively sitting, waiting for him to drop the money in our laps, as we say, "I'm praying and waiting."

But that is *not* the word, as faith without work is dead. If you don't participate in your own blessing, you better call a mortician and plan the funeral for your success, because your faith is dead.

Idle chatter produces poverty, they say, so stop talking and start walking.

Biography

Fitz P. Mombeleur is living proof that it makes no difference where you start in life; anyone can have the life of his or her dreams. He is a husband, chef, business owner, pastor, life coach, financial guru, and a popular public speaker.

Fitz P. Mombeleur

Growing up on the streets of New York City, Fitz learned the value of hard work, persistence and how to get things done even in the face of much opposition and criticism.

Straight from high school, Fitz began a successful career with several large, prestigious financial organizations including Chase Bank, Wells Fargo, Omni American, and CitiMortgage. It became clear to him there was more to life than cubicles and trading time for dollars. Despite his own fears and his family's persuasive arguments against the change, Fitz turned his back on corporate America to pursue full-time ministry.

His mission is to help families enjoy health, wealth, prosperity, and happiness, which is what motivated Fitz and his wife, Fabiola, to start GAP International Ministries in Addison, Texas. They also founded a for-profit marriage coaching business: L.O.V.E. (Living Our Vows Every day), which hosts sessions across the Dallas-Fort Worth metroplex to help couples understand their new responsibilities as they prepare to be married.

Fitz and Fabiola have a beautiful four-year-old foster daughter and an amazing dog named Boguz.

Fitz is in the process of writing *Life after Death*, the first of many planned books. He also speaks to new audiences as often as he can, and he is devoted to training and inspiring the next generation to be leaders as well as better husbands and wives. He always includes his favorite saying: "You are responsible for your life."

Contact Information

Email: info@fitzmotivates.com
Website: fitzmotivativates.com
Instagram: @pstrfitz
Twitter: @fitzspeaks
LinkedIn: fitz-p-mombeleur-3809a3a5

CHAPTER FIVE

Make the Journey Unforgettable

Petros Mitsides

My career in track and field was launched by a teasing comment my physical education teacher made twenty-nine years ago, a light joke that sparked my love for a sport. Since then, my passion has been training and competing in the discus throw, the shot put, and the hammer throw. I consider my greatest achievements winning four gold medals and three silver medals at the World Masters Athletics Championships, winning four gold medals at the European Masters Athletics Championships, competing in six finals at the Commonwealth Games, and being Cyprus National Champion eight times.

In the course of our lives, a handful of opportunities present themselves to us. If we choose to pursue them, they are life-changing, even though we might not realize it at the time. My big opportunity presented itself when I was twelve.

When I was two years old, my Greek Cypriot family moved from Cyprus to London because of my father's work. I was always interested in sports and I really enjoyed participating in almost anything that was competitive, so I played soccer, rugby, cricket, basketball, and swam. During the track and field season the spring I turned twelve, I noticed a couple of my friends throwing the discus and shot put, and it looked like fun. When my physical education teacher said, "You're Greek, so you should be able to throw the discus," I decided to give it a try. He was probably teasing me, but it really made an impact.

Believe in yourself and avoid negative self-talk. If you don't believe in yourself, you have already set yourself up to run into a brick wall.

Just those few words of encouragement motivated me, and a couple of weeks later, I was taking part in a track and field competition with schools from the London area. I competed in my age group in the discus throw and the shot put and managed to come first and fourth respectively. That was it for me—that first competition made me really fall in love with the sport.

We moved back to Cyprus later that year, I began training in the sport, and my dream started to grow. My ultimate goal was to compete at the Olympic Games, as it is with most good athletes, and even at that young age, I was very determined, committed, and willing to put in the time and effort that was needed to make my dream a reality.

Most people say that to achieve your goals you need to make sacrifices, but is this really the case? Yes, it is true that you need to give up a few things in your life, but instead of thinking of it as a sacrifice, it is more helpful to treat it as better time management and spending more time focusing on the activities which will allow you to reach your dreams. And always try to keep it fun!

There will always be struggles and obstacles along the way, but those are what make the story more exhilarating and make your accomplishments even more meaningful, so enjoy the journey!

High school was relatively straightforward. I trained at the stadium for two to three hours after school, six days a week. I was blessed with the support of both my parents, whether it was driving me daily to the stadium for training, showing up to all my competitions, or just some simple words of encouragement.

I have never been the most naturally talented, strongest, tallest, or fastest thrower. I am around six feet, three inches/190 centimeters tall, but most of the successful athletes in the throwing events are a lot taller and much stronger. Where I excelled, however, was in my work ethic, dedication, and determination, and I *always* trained and competed clean. In addition, what I lacked in physical strength and speed, I made up for with excellent technique.

My first major life obstacle presented itself immediately after high school. In Cyprus, men have mandatory military service as soon as they finish high school, so for two years of my life, training was definitely hindered. Because of my athletic performances and good results, I was permitted a few hours every day to train, but considering the late teenage years are the peak training years of an athlete's career, those hours were nowhere near enough.

Above all, make it fun and enjoy the journey. Fulfilling your dreams is never easy, but it's not impossible either.

My biggest challenge was finding the energy and determination to train after all the army commitments of the day, and with only about three to four hours of sleep every night. I guess at that age everything is possible, because even though I felt like a zombie for those two years, I kept my ultimate goal in mind and was able to push through the fatigue, the lack of sleep, and the stress of the military. Giving up is never an option for me; I am more stubborn than that.

When it was time to apply to university, I made the choice to study in the United States; I had lived in the United Kingdom for eleven years and in Cyprus for nine years, and decided it was time to experience something new. I applied to quite a few universities and colleges, and was even offered a full athletic scholarship, but I wanted to go to a university that offered an outstanding academic program, had a great track and field throwing coach, and included other world class athletes. I decided to go to Dallas, Texas, and attend Southern Methodist University (SMU), which had two discus throwers who made the finals of the World Championships the previous year. Even though attending SMU would place a greater financial burden on my family, it was probably the wisest decision I made because it increased the likelihood of me improving and reaching my goals.

I really enjoyed my time in college—which is why I went back to SMU for my MBA—and although a lot of students complain that there isn't enough time, it really *is* all about time management and organization.

I was lucky enough to figure out early on that there is a simple formula for succeeding in pretty much anything you want to accomplish in life.

Common sense suggests you need to put in the hours, days, and perhaps even years to accomplish your goals. However, being focused and being as productive as possible during that time is probably just as important, if not more so. Proper training is critical as well, so listen to and follow people who have been successful in the area in which you hope to excel.

Getting a college degree was definitely important to me, but there were other things I cared about more. I guess it helped that some of my strongest attributes are organization and focus, which is probably due to my many years in athletics and my military service. I made sure that I didn't skip any classes, and while I was in class, I paid attention and took good notes.

Maintaining that discipline saved me a lot of time studying outside of class and helped me make the honor roll every semester. It also freed up enough time to do the things I was passionate about: training and competing in my sport, hanging out with friends, and helping other students by being a teaching assistant/graduate assistant.

Even though I was pretty much on track and doing the right things, not everything came easy. Because I chose to attend a university which already had star athletes—some of whom had already competed in the Olympic Games and World Championships—I felt somewhat neglected by my coach during my freshman year.

With the benefit of hindsight, I understand a coach would focus on the most productive and more talented people, but at the time, I felt I was being ignored. Now I realize it was probably the best thing that could have happened.

The throwing events in track and field are extremely technical and there are two ways you can approach them. You can either be passive and wait for your coach to tell you what you are doing right or wrong, or you can be proactive and start paying attention to what you are doing, what you are feeling, and start correcting yourself. I chose the proactive approach, and by focusing, putting in more effort, and working even harder, I improved dramatically and earned my coach's approval and attention.

This major lesson has helped me in all aspects of my life. If you want to succeed in something, it's up to you to get it done. Don't expect someone else to do the heavy lifting for you! It seems counterintuitive, but I've learned this is true: You don't usually get to choose your mentor or coach. They choose *you* when you are ready.

I faced some other major barriers throughout my journey. Track and field is not as lucrative for athletes as football, soccer, or basketball, even if you are one of the top athletes in the world in your event. To survive, most of us must have a job. This was the case for me also, so instead of putting in four to six hours of training a day, I was only able to train around three hours a day after work.

Another obstacle was a serious shoulder problem that had been misdiagnosed for more than a decade. I finally managed to get the shoulder fixed when I was 29. Had the injury been diagnosed correctly and had I undergone surgery when I was younger, things might have turned out even better.

I was never discouraged.

Though I may not have made the Olympic team for my country, I did compete in and have done well in other major global events. I was honored to represent Cyprus in three Commonwealth Games—a major competition held every four years with more than seventy participating countries including Canada, United Kingdom, Australia, India, Jamaica, and South Africa—and I made six finals in three different throwing events.

I also won the Cyprus National Athletics Championships eight times and held the national discus record for five years.

Toward the end of my peak years, other athletes

and friends sometimes advised me I should quit while I was in top shape and still doing pretty well. I refused to listen. I enjoyed what I was doing, and even though it's always great to win, just being in the game has always been enough reward in itself. Even though I was getting older and I wasn't in my best physical condition with a few injuries here and there, and even though there were people encouraging me to call it quits, I still decided to *push on*. I figured I had decades of experience, my technique was still decent, and I was enjoying what I was doing.

My decision to push on was vindicated when I was 36 and competed in my first Masters Games, a competition where the minimum age of eligibility is 35. My first competition was the European Masters Athletics Championships in Izmir, Turkey, and I won four gold medals in the four throwing events in which I competed. For the first few moments after the competition, it felt anticlimactic because winning in all four events seemed a little too easy.

Then it dawned on me: The reason why it seemed easy was because I have spent years developing the skill, the strength, and the technique. I also had the experience and the mindset that made the victory seem easier than it was.

My experience was similar to the well-known Pablo Picasso anecdote. When a woman asked Picasso to draw her, he took only a few seconds to create the perfect sketch, and then he told her the cost was $5,000. When the woman asked why so much money for something that had taken him only a few seconds to draw, Picasso told her she was wrong—it had taken him his entire life.

Since then I have competed in three different World Masters Athletics Championships, winning another four gold medals and three silver medals. The Masters competitions may not be as prestigious or as commercialized as the Olympic Games, but they are still global events, and I consider my results major achievements.

So, what does success mean? Even though I wasn't able to achieve my ultimate goal of competing in the Olympic Games, I am very happy and proud of my achievements and all the hard work that I put in, even the struggles I went through.

My definition of success has evolved. Now:

- *Success* is hearing my national anthem played in my honor eight times at major international championships.
- *Success* is having won gold and silver medals at the Masters World Championships and making it to six finals at the Commonwealth Games.
- *Success* is traveling to countries all around the world through my competitions and my work.
- *Success* is having the confidence to easily interact with the many good friends I have made from dozens of countries, who respect what I have accomplished and the person I have become, and to carry this confidence into all my non-sport interactions.
- *Success* is when other athletes come to me and ask for advice on their technique even though they may have better personal bests than I do.
- *Success* is when the Australian TV presenters (during the Melbourne Commonwealth Games in 2006)

acknowledge my dedication and love for the sport by commenting in the live broadcast, after my third final of the championships: *That will be the end of the campaign for Petros Mitsides of Cyprus. He's had a great meet here; he's competed in all the throwing events bar the javelin. He just loves throwing, obviously.*

- *Success* is applying the determination and drive I practiced in my athletic career to become an entrepreneur, a musician, a photographer and to develop other non-sports-related skills.

- *Success* is applying the discipline acquired through sports to enhance my professional career, and having the right mindset to deal with life's challenges and opportunities with confidence and belief that I can persevere and succeed in anything I put my mind to.

If you keep working toward your dreams and never give up, success is bound to happen, even though it might be framed a little differently than you originally imagined. Being able to be proud of your hard work and accomplishments and earning respect for your efforts is definitely worth the journey.

To succeed at anything in life, you need to pay attention and be passionate. Although I was probably more talented in music than in athletics, I had greater accomplishments in sports because that's what I loved and where I put in most of my time and effort.

Believe in yourself and avoid negative self-talk. If you don't believe, you have already set yourself up to run into a brick wall. I was blessed to have friends and family encouraging me along the way; their support has been a major factor as to why I have been able to do well.

Even if you haven't been fortunate enough to have people in your life encouraging and supporting you, be a beacon of light for your children, your family, and your friends. A little encouragement can go a long way (remember my teacher's comment about Greek athletes and the discus throw). And who knows, you may even start having more faith in yourself. Always be humble and work hard, and let your results do the talking for you.

Above all, make it fun and enjoy the journey. Fulfilling your dreams is never easy, but it's not impossible either. All that is needed is dedication, time, persistence, hard work, and belief.

Biography

Petros Mitsides has a broad range of interests and exceptional skills. Representing Cyprus, he is a Masters Athletics World Champion, and he is also an entrepreneur, marketeer, musician, and a photographer.

Petros Mitsides

Born in Cyprus and raised there and in London, he served his military duty as a corporal in the Cyprus army before moving to the United States for college. At Southern

Methodist University, he graduated with Magna Cum Laude in Marketing and Economics while he competed in college track and field, and later earned an MBA with honors.

Petros has put his degrees to good use with his executive marketing position at Ermes Group, the largest and most diversified retailer in Cyprus, and uses his entrepreneurial skills as a travel company independent representative.

His track and field accomplishments are exceptional: Four gold and three silver medals in the World Masters Athletics Championships, four gold medals in the European Masters Athletics Championships, former Cyprus record-holder and eight-time national champion in the hammer throw, discus throw, and shot put.

A talented keyboard/piano musician, Petros also is a professional-level marketeer and sporting event photographer, especially for events sponsored by the Cyprus Amateur Athletics Association and GSP Sports Complex in Nicosia, where he lives when he's not traveling around the world.

Contact information

Email: petros.mitsides@gmail.com
Facebook: www.facebook.com/peter.mitsides

CHAPTER SIX

The 'Secret' of Success

Matt Morris

I was blessed to have the secret of success put into my hands when I was just 18 years old. The secret came in the form of a book, *Think and Grow Rich,* a classic written in 1937 by Napoleon Hill.

As I opened the book and eagerly began reading, the first words I saw were a promise: *In this book lies the secret of success.*

I was thrilled; I had dreamed my entire life of becoming rich. The book I was reading was the compilation of wealth strategies from 400 of the richest people in the world.

My mind raced as I read through the pages. Napoleon Hill promised he was going to share the secret. Because this was the first self-improvement book I'd ever read, somewhere in my mind I visualized there was one specific place in the book where he would carefully spell out the mysterious secret of success.

I was determined not to miss this all-important page.

Over the next several days I read the entire book, and while I loved the content, I was incredibly frustrated. *Nowhere* in the book did he reveal the secret.

My mind must have wandered and was tuned out on the page where he revealed this secret, I thought to myself.

I don't care what excuse you may have; I've seen others with much bigger excuses overcome their challenges and achieve their goals.

Over the next week or two, I read the book again with a fine-tooth comb, carefully searching for the exact words, *The secret of success is . . . .*

I was looking for the magic bullet, the ONE strategy that, if carefully followed, would lead me to the land of milk and honey, showering me with untold riches.

But once again I came to the final page with never once being told this single mysterious secret.

I was frustrated. Even a little pissed off. Was the promise in the beginning of the book just a clever marketing ploy to get people to read the book?

Or maybe . . . could it be possible . . . he meant the secret lies within this book, but I must determine for myself what that secret is?

I put my frustration aside and decided to go with the harder option.

So, with highlighter in hand, I saddled myself up to read the book the *third* time with the goal of making my own conclusion as to what the secret really is.

When I had finished the book for the third time, I realized something profound. Among all the incredible success stories, there was no single common strategy that these successful men and women had used. There was *no* common strategy. *No* secret tactic. *No* magic pixie dust.

The ONLY thing stopping you is a lack of determination.

All those profiled in the book had struggled mightily, but they realized their success because of one word.

After 24 years as an entrepreneur, generating over $1,000,000,000 in sales through my companies and sales organizations, speaking to audiences of hundreds of thousands of people around the world, and mentoring more than fifty others to become million-dollar earners, only one word still comes to mind as the secret to success.

That word is *determination*.

Very simply said, the man or woman who has the courage to never give up and continue working relentlessly and persistently on their goals will reach them.

I don't care what excuse you may have; I've seen others with much bigger excuses overcome their challenges and achieve their goals.

After I've helped so many thousands of people achieve financial freedom, I am positive you DO have what it takes to achieve this same success for yourself.

The ONLY thing stopping you is a lack of determination.

You may not currently have the knowledge to succeed in whatever career path you chose, but if you have determination, you'll get the knowledge.

You may not have the sales or people skills to succeed, but if you have determination, you'll learn those skills.

You may be afraid of people, have a fear of rejection, and be deathly afraid of speaking in public, but if you have determination, you'll overcome those fears.

You may have been born in a third-world country, raised in abject poverty, and feel like a prisoner to your circumstances, but if you have determination, you'll fight your way out.

You cannot convince me you do not have everything it takes to find a way to succeed if—and *only* if—you have the determination to win.

How am I so certain?

Because I have seen countless others have all of those excuses, and too many other excuses to mention, and succeed anyway.

In life, you either fight for your excuses or you fight for your success. You get what you focus on.

If you allow your mind to let your limitations be an excuse, you will fail.

If, however, you refuse to let your limitations be an excuse, you will win.

Success is as simple as that.

Yes, there will be a myriad of tactics and strategies you'll need to implement, and there will be many skills you will have to learn.

With determination, you will figure all of that out.

Without determination, you will make excuses and quit.

There will be times when you get down on yourself.

In life, you either fight for your excuses or you fight for your success. You get what you focus on.

There will be times when you fail.

There will be times when you are betrayed.

There will be times when you get rejected.

There will be times where you can't even see a path forward.

There will be times when you will lie to yourself, making up excuses to justify quitting.

But with determination, you will continue forward relentlessly in the direction of your dreams, despite all of those obstacles.

With determination, you will *always* find a way over, around, or through any obstacle that gets in your way.

With determination, you will never, EVER give up on your dreams.

With determination, you will do today what others won't, to have tomorrow what others don't.

Mark my words, you will struggle.

It will be hard at times.

But with persistence and determination, you will succeed.

I'll share with you a quote that I read daily during the times I went through periods of struggle. This quote, plus my rock-solid belief in everything I've shared with you in this chapter, have carried me through the lowest of lows. This is what has allowed me to experience a life filled with fulfillment, significance, success, and pure joy.

Far better is it to dare mighty things, to win glorious triumphs, even though checkered by failure... than to rank with those poor spirits who neither enjoy nor suffer much, because they live in a gray twilight that knows not victory nor defeat.

—Theodore Roosevelt

Biography

Matt Morris

By the time Matt Morris was thirteen, his father had been sent to prison for murder, had become an alcoholic, and had committed suicide. Matt credits his single mother as his biggest inspiration; as she raised him by herself, she worked two and three jobs at a time and completed college and law school.

Matt started his own business when he was just eighteen, but by the time he was 21, he was $30,000 in debt, homeless, and living in his beat-up Honda Civic. Two months of sleeping in his car and bathing in gas station bathrooms inspired Matt to radically re-invent his life.

Through a massive commitment to personal development and disciplined work ethic, by the time he was 24 he was earning a six-figure income, and by 29 he was a self-made millionaire. Now with more than 24 years' experience as a top network marketing trainer and leader, Matt has built sales organizations that have generated well over one million customers, producing in excess of $1 billion in sales.

A self-admitted adventure junkie, he has traveled to more than 70 countries around the world and checked off 80 accomplishments on his bucket list, which include climbing Mount Kilimanjaro, cage diving with great white sharks, paragliding, skydiving, racing camels around the Great Pyramids in Egypt, hiking to Machu Picchu, zip lining at Victoria Falls in Zimbabwe, riding a hot air balloon in Africa above the running of the wildebeests, and white-water rafting in the Andes.

He's had ten books on the bestseller lists; his number-one bestseller is *The Unemployed Millionaire: Escape the Rat Race, Fire Your Boss and Live Life on YOUR Terms!*

Matt has been interviewed nationally and internationally on television and radio, including ABC, CBS, NBC, Fox News, and CNN.

He regularly speaks to audiences numbering in the thousands and has spoken in 25 countries. His story of overcoming adversity makes him one of the most authentic, dynamic, and inspirational speakers in the world.

Matt is the proud father of three beautiful children.

Contact information

Website: MattMorris.com
Facebook: MattMorrisAdventure
Instagram: @MattMorrisadventure
Twitter: @matthewdmorris
YouTube: matthewdmorris
Snapchat: adventurematt

CHAPTER SEVEN

Becoming Your True Self

Christopher Henderson, Sr.

"It's always been like this."
"It's not going to get any better."
"I guess I'm just supposed to be overweight."
"I'm too old now."
"I never finished college."
"I know God can, but I really don't think He will . . . not for me, anyway."
"I'll try, but it just won't work out."
"I just can't."

Are you like me? For as long as I remember, at least one of those negative, self-loathing thoughts raced through my brain. For as long as I remember, feelings of incompetence, inability, and insufficiency ruled my mind.

As a teenager, I had been a fit athlete preparing to enter the Air Force Academy. Years later, I consoled myself by saying, "Well, round is a shape, so I must be in shape!"

I entertained moments of temporary success, but the scales too often tipped toward the negative. In my heart, there was always an inescapable, undeniable yearning for what I believed still could be, but I had to acknowledge the

---

If you are working on becoming a better version of yourself, you should have an image of who you want to be and what you want to accomplish.

---

disheartening truth: I had become accustomed to failure, not just the *feeling* of failure, but more painfully, the *acceptance* of failure. Deep inside, I knew I was still laden with potential; but being brutally honest, I had become a perpetual *"almost."*

- I *almost* made it to the Air Force Academy.
- I *almost* had the relationship of my dreams.
- I *almost* was a successful entrepreneur.
- I *almost* made it to 15% body fat.
- I *almost* was the dad I wanted to be.
- I *almost* was the person I wanted to be.

And *then* . . .

I looked at *everything*. I looked at my bank account, my love handles, my relationships, my very life; and *I decided that I was better than what I had become.* After two decades of minimal success and maximal frustration, I applied myself to change my life. The revelation that moved me to change my world came when I learned one simple truth:

I had to *become*. Again.

I had *become* what I was. I realized *to change my life experience, I had to BECOME all over again*. Start over. Anew. Ground Zero.

I now share with you the process I used to . . . **become**.

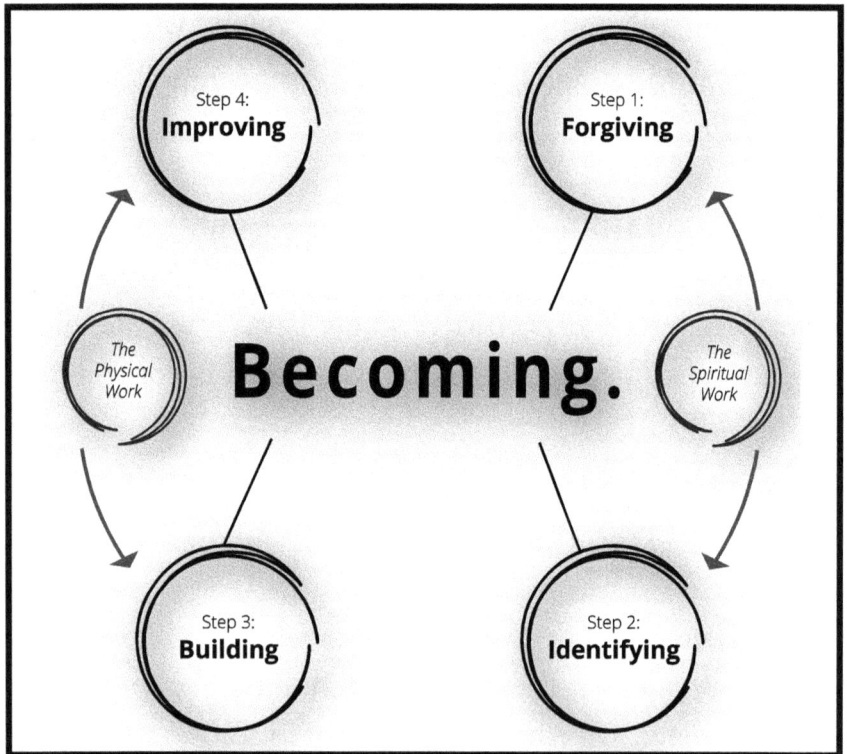

Step 1: Forgiving

The first (and hardest) thing I had to do in order to *become* again was to forgive. When we think of forgiveness, our mental hard drive usually retrieves the files of all the people who have hurt or wronged us. I was no different. I often replayed the memories of those times when life seemed unfair because of what others had done.

I was buried under the bitterness of my past. It manifested itself in low esteem and the inability to capitalize on real opportunities. I came to realize, if I ever wanted to experience a fulfilling life, I had to forgive. I had to consciously, intentionally go back in my past and forgive the number one person who wronged me. No, it wasn't anyone in my family, nor was it a person from any previous relationship. My breakthrough came when I realized I had to forgive . . . *myself.*

I, like too many, had the tendency to blame others for the condition of my life. I even blamed God. One night, I went to church after midnight to go *"Creed vs. Drago"* with the Lord. I was ready to unleash my raw, unfiltered anger; but as soon as I was prepared for Round One, these words resonated within me:

"Why did you give away your strength?"

Silence.

Before I could get my first punch in, I realized God had not put me in the situation I was in. It was none other than (yes, you guessed it)—me.

Instinctively, I fought the truth:

But this person did me wrong! It wasn't my fault!

But that person lied about me! It wasn't my fault!

But this person went behind my back! It wasn't my fault!

Those were my immediate thoughts. I realized my reaction to the truth was *to give power to everyone else.* I then understood a fundamental truth: if I ever wanted to break free of bitterness, I had to accept and internalize that God's power inside me was greater than *any* influence outside me. The person who did me the greatest harm was *the same person* who made the decision to participate in the negative scenarios in the first place. True, there were people I needed to forgive, but freedom from my past only came when I took personal ownership of what I had become.

No longer would I *ever* cede my power to any other person for any reason.

I forgave myself for not using my strength and consequently, for the unwise decisions I had made.

Forgiving myself was the hardest thing to do because it forced me to accept my own truth: I was *where* I was because I was *who* I was. Taking this first step was simultaneously liberating and empowering. Learning personal forgiveness and leaving bitterness behind prepared me for the second step in the *becoming* process, and that is . . .

STEP 2: IDENTIFYING

One of the fundamental realities of all creation is the natural proclivity to reproduce. Mankind is the only species that doesn't reproduce as a matter of natural course. Most every other living thing reproduces and behaves instinctively. Elementary, you say? I concede that.

Even more rudimentary, all living things naturally exemplify the characteristics of their order. When alligators hatch, they already know to swim and to perform the "death roll." When butterflies escape their cocoons, they instinctively know to fly and to scan for nectar. These phenomena exist in nature for one reason—*the identity and function of the creation are inextricably tied to the source of the One who created it.*

Before we identify who we are to become, it is necessarily important that we first identify the nature of our creation. The true essence of every human is spiritual, and this truth gives us insight. We naturally aspire for greatness because the Source of our creation is naturally great. We yearn for fulfillment because it is a natural, God-inspired characteristic of our very being.

This is why the second step to *becoming* is *identifying.* As we identify our true nature, we discover who we are called to become and what we are called to do. This stage of the process answers the questions:

- What is my purpose?
- What is my vision?
- How can I contribute to my generation?
- Which are my unique passions and capabilities?
- What must I accomplish?

These introspective questions are essential in the process of identifying who we truly are. Until we can answer these questions with transparency, *becoming* something new will be forever elusive. The answers to these questions lead to fulfillment and significance because our Creator works through purpose and intention.

Identifying also involves deciding to become different. "Deciding" is a remarkably challenging word, because it literally means "to remove, to cut off." Consider similar words with the same root:

- Sui-cide: to cut off one's own life
- Homi-cide: to cut off the life of another
- Geno-cide: to cut off the life of a people or culture

What do all these words have in common? That's right, the concept of *permanent removal*. When we make a decision, when we truly *decide*, we are removing all other options. Once something is permanently removed, it *never comes back*. Once we identify the person we want to become and make a decision to become that person, we permanently remove the option of staying the same!

Our old habits, our former thought processes, and our previous behavior patterns are removed, never to come back again. Therefore, when we start a new process (i.e., losing weight, adhering to a budget, or pursuing our education), but then completely give up, we have to honestly question if we made a true, real decision. *When we truly make a decision, we remove the option of going back to our former actions or habits.* This level of commitment allows us to grasp what we are truly able to do: to identify not only our purpose, but also our gifts and capabilities that allow us to work diligently to make our purpose come alive.

After we have forgiven ourselves and identified who we are to become, we are ready for the next step.

STEP 3: WORKING

Now it's time to roll up our sleeves and go to work.

Yes, *work*.

Inherent in the concept of work is the mental image of a finished product. In the mind, the work is already finished because there is a definite, concrete final outcome, even if it only exists in theory.

- If you are detailing your car, what does the final product look like?
- If you are preparing a meal, what does the final product look like?

When you think of these tasks, you can create a mental image of each one of them completed. Now I present another question:

If you are working on YOU, what does YOUR final product look like?

Consider this analogy: When I was a child, I was addicted to large jigsaw puzzles. I loved to put the outside frame together first, but it didn't take me long to realize that the most important part of the process was not the frame. It wasn't even the *pieces* of the puzzle. The most important part of the process was *the picture on the box*! The box showed what the final product looked like. It demonstrated how all the pieces of the puzzle connect to produce order and meaning.

If you are working on *becoming* a better version of yourself, you should have an image of who you want to be and what you want to accomplish. Once you envision the final product, *now* is the time to start the work. *Working* is essential to *becoming*. Without work, your image of the final product remains in the realm of wishful thinking. We now craft, mold, shape, and hone. We work relentlessly at *becoming* the person we've always known we can be, the person we each are destined to become.

Unfortunately, I believe this third step is the phase where many people tend to become ambivalent or apathetic regarding their personal growth. Why? Because it's hard and produces sweat! It produces discomfort or pain. *(Side note: Don't expect to have great change without great pain!)* Work is hard because there are so many forces that vie for our focus. There will either be a complete focus on *becoming*, or our focus will invariably drift toward remaining the same. Both ideals cannot coexist in the same space.

Knowing *what* to do is never the primary issue. *Doing what needs to be done with focus, commitment, and consistency* is the real challenge.

GET AT IT.

Now, let's explore five practical tasks to help us in our quest to *become*:

1. Write in specific detail what your finished picture looks like. If you want to have the best marriage in the world, define what a "great marriage" is. The same applies to increasing your net worth or being a better parent. Having a clear perception of what you are *becoming* is fundamental to the process. (Remember, you need to know what the puzzle box cover looks like!)

2. Find a mentor who is skilled and successful at what you are working toward. The shortest path to success is not trial and error. *Experience is the best teacher* is a common maxim, though not necessarily accurate. *Other people's experiences are the best teachers* is far superior, because others have already made the mistakes and discovered strategies for success. Search them out, listen, and implement their counsel.

3. Eliminate your personal distractions. Get out of bed. Limit your phone use, television, and social media. These diversions lead us to lose track of our most critical re-source—time. Of all the assets you have at your disposal, time is the one thing you cannot replace once it is spent.

4. Get to work. No thinking, no pondering, no medi-tating, no questioning. Start writing. Get your rear-end to that gym. Get on the website, enroll in that class, and start studying. Pick up the phone and set the meeting with your potential client. Whatever your task is, GET. TO. WORK. As Solomon stated in Ecclesiastes 9:10, *"Whatever your hand finds to do, do it with all your might . . ."* Enough said.

5. Evaluate your progress with periodic checkpoints. If you are leaving Dallas for Oklahoma, make sure you fol-low the signs that say "north." Life will always give us signs that we are headed in the right direction. Compare your progress with the image of your future self. Continually ensure you're on the right road.

Working is an integral part of the *becoming* process. Without work, forgiving and identifying are forever the-oretical; and theory alone never produces tangible results. Once you have been consistent in this third step, you now must do one more thing; and you must do it continually.

STEP 4: IMPROVING.

You have progressed this far.

I congratulate you for courageously reaching back into your past and forgiving yourself. You have released your bitterness. You have taken ownership of your decisions, and you recognize that there is no human on this planet that has more power over your life than you do.

I congratulate and commend you for doing the intro-spective search into your soul to identify who you are and what you are supposed to *become*. It may seem as though you are nowhere close to becoming *that* person and living *that* life, but you own the insight of your real truth—the truth of knowing that there is so, so much more inside of you than what you are manifesting at this moment.

I congratulate and commend you for making the deci-sion to work harder for yourself than you do for any other person. You are now taking active, purposeful steps every day to become the person that you have identified. You made up your mind, and you actually worked to *become* your new self.

> ***For these steps you have taken,***
> ***from my heart I congratulate and commend you.***

There is one more step for you to *become* fully who you are destined to be. ***That step is committing yourself to never, ever, ever going back spiritually, emotionally, mentally, or physically to what you have left behind.***

There are many scriptural examples of making a com-mitment to continually improve: Proverbs 26:11, St. Mat-thew 12:43-45, St. John 8-10,11, and St. John 5-14 are a few personal favorites because they speak of never going back to what you once were. One of the worst mistakes we can make is going backward after making the decision to re-create ourselves.

If you have decided to *become*, that decision is the door that guards your mind. Doors keep intruders outside and prized possessions inside. The state of mind that impris-oned you before you forgave yourself is an unwanted intruder, and it now forever remains *outside* your door. The incredible power of truth resides *inside*, the real truth about who you are and what you are actually able to do.

Lock the door, and never let those undesired, incapacitating thoughts enter your spiritual/mental/emotional/physical residence again.

Ever.

We're not finished. We must protect the metaphorical door of our minds by drastically limiting or completely avoiding:

- Companions who refuse to grow and walk with us in our new journey.
- Previous environments that present too much temptation to regress to what we once were.
- Habits that enslaved us, overpowered us, and sought to kill our potential.

These must stay outside the door, and that door must be locked with a deadbolt, padlock, and a steel chain. Never allow such malevolence inside. In their place, we now embrace:

- Positive mentors who coach us with absolute honesty and like-minded mentality.
- Venues, meetings, conferences, and seminars that fill us with a mindset of success.
- New, empowering practices (prayer, proper nutrition, exercise, and reading) to condition our mind and body to live with renewed energy and enthusiasm. These are also protected inside the door as we consciously safeguard our new thought processes for the remainder of our lives.

Forgive. Identify. Work. Improve.

BECOME.

The manacles that imprison the mind are not mandatory, but voluntary. One who desires liberation must first desire illumination, for the keys that would free the mind are not about us in well-lit surroundings, but within us in the obscure, opaque chambers of the unyielded heart.

Biography

Christopher Henderson, Sr., of DeSoto, Texas, is a graduate of Texas A&M University. A student leader and a member of the Aggie football team, he majored in Speech Communication and minored in Spanish.

After 13 years in corporate leadership, Chris became an educator, teaching high school Spanish. He is an accomplished public speaker in education and personal development, a licensed financial professional, and is lead pastor of Star of Hope Church in DeSoto.

Christopher Henderson, Sr.

Contact information:

Email:　　chris@christophersherard.com
Website:　www.christophersherard.com
Facebook: christophersherardbecome
Twitter:　@csbecome

CHAPTER EIGHT

In the 'No'

Candice Bolek

Rejection. We face it every single day. Your work proposal gets shot down. Your spouse vetoes the paint color you love. Your credit card is declined. When these things happen, we don't typically drop everything and run for the rooftops shouting, "I've been rejected!" In most cases, we just take a breath and move on.

There is a staggering amount of rejection that comes with being an actress. Sometimes when people ask me what I do for a living, I want to respond with, "I'm a professional rejection-taker."

There are days when I get rejected so much that I wonder if I'm walking around in life with a Post-it Note on my forehead that reads, "Reject me."

Mostly, though, I'm just grateful to be walking around in life.

The doctor almost killed us both.

That is how my mom describes my birth. I was born via emergency C-section, and my dad tells me I was blue from oxygen deprivation when I was removed from my mom's abdomen.

In the acting world, I am what's known as "ethnically ambiguous." It's the politically correct way of saying, "No one can tell what ethnicity you are." Imagine the confusion if I could also be mistaken for Smurf.

I've stayed the course even in those times when it seemed like quitting was my only option.

Alas, I wasn't blue for long. My flesh-toned color returned just in time for my parents to get the news I had a ventricular septal defect (hole in the heart). While not necessarily life-threatening, the hole meant I would need annual echo cardiograms to monitor my condition. I also had to take antibiotics prior to routine dental visits to prevent possible infection from traveling to my heart.

Thank God I was given a name that starts with "Can."

I have seen numerous variations and misspellings of my name over the years, one of which is "Candance." Yes, I know I can dance. In fact, I grew up dancing. For eight years, I studied jazz, tap, and ballet. This included multiple classes a week, annual dance recitals, community performances, and competitions.

I suppose it's not that big of a leap from being a dancer to having an interest in acting. I was already a natural performer, happy to be on stage. My obsession with Tom Cruise right around puberty put Hollywood on my radar. Talk about *take my breath away*! I watched *Top Gun* repeatedly. Naturally, in order to meet him, I had no choice but to go to Los Angeles and become an actress.

I am only half joking about that.

And move to Los Angeles I did! In 2001, nearly two years after graduating from college, I left Bowling Green, Kentucky, for California. The fact that I had zero acting experience or training whatsoever didn't deter me in the slightest, but you can imagine my chosen path raised some eyebrows among my friends and family. My poor dad. The man so generously paid for my college education only for me to run off to LA to become an actress. I don't think that's what he had in mind for his *magna cum laude* graduate daughter. Even today, when I walk out of auditions I sometimes think, "Thank you, Dad," and "I'm sorry."

When you throw caution to the wind to pursue your dream, the wind, in response, may blow some things your way you didn't anticipate.

Enter sacrifice.

Living 2,400 miles away from home means missing out on a lot of occasions—weddings, bachelorette parties, birthdays, baby showers, funerals—you name it. The financial struggle is real. I got my feet wet in "the biz" as an extra making minimum wage. I've taken jobs that didn't pay particularly well because they offered the flexibility to audition and work on set. Then there's the cost of running my business: headshots, classes and gas, oh my! LA, itself, isn't cheap. I swear I pay for the sun in my rent. What else? Oh, yeah. The rejection.

But don't cry for me, Argentina. The truth is, I can only hear "No" if I'm in the line of fire, and by line of fire, I mean at an audition with a camera pointed at me. You see, it's practically a miracle if I even get an audition. Thousands of actors are submitted for a role, 50-60 will get the audition, and only one will book the job. The odds are not in my favor. From a pure numbers' standpoint, they never are. It's a privilege to be called into that room, and in that vein, I guess it's a privilege to be rejected.

When you throw caution to the wind to pursue your dream, the wind, in response, may blow some things your way you didn't anticipate.

If you're a salesperson, you can separate yourself from the product you're selling to some extent. As an actor, *you* are the product. There is no separating the two. Not getting the callback or not booking the job is like hearing, "We don't like YOU. We don't need YOU. We don't want YOU. We already have someone just like YOU." And, it's not personal! I've been too white, too ethnic, too short, too tall, too pretty, not pretty enough, too young, too old—you get the gist. And heaven help me if I look like the director's ex-wife. I have little to no control over this process, so I mind my P's and my . . . other P's—professionalism and performance. Did I mention you have to have thick skin to be an actress? By now, I'd say I'm bulletproof.

I am not, however, gluten-proof. Of all the rejections I've faced, there's been none more painful than the one I received from my own body. In 2014, I was diagnosed with celiac disease. The disease is far beyond a gluten allergy or sensitivity; it is a straight-up autoimmune disorder.

Fourteen years into this journey, and it was the first time my brain seriously considered choosing a different path. Luckily, my heart has a mind of its own.

A gastroenterologist confirmed the diagnosis with an endoscopy. He lowered a tube down my throat and into my gut, where he took a biopsy of my small intestine and sent it off to the lab for examination. Before I was sedated, I asked him what the odds were that my biopsy results would be negative. He quickly responded, "Zero." Great. Nothing like wasting my time and money submitting myself to an unnecessary medical procedure.

But wait! There's more.

"When you go gluten-free, you can expect to gain 25 to 30 pounds. It's not a big deal," he explained.

I was horrified.

"It *is* a big deal to me, especially in my profession."

"What do you do?"

"I'm an actress, and I do some modeling."

"Well, just don't go sticking your finger down your throat."

Fade to black.

Despite having just been sedated, I couldn't sleep that night for fear my body would become unrecognizable, and my acting career would be over because of it.

No. It was bleaker than that. My *life* as I knew it would be over.

My intestines were so damaged that Dr. Sensitive didn't even need the biopsy results to confirm the celiac diagnosis. It was a blow for sure. With celiac disease, continuing to eat the wrong food, even something as small as a Tic Tac, could send me to an early grave.

Aside from the serious business of needing to stay alive, this unwelcome illness has cost me some bookings. I once crushed a callback for a Pizza Hut commercial, but did I book it? No. I can't eat the product! I've been to a few castings where I was expected to eat bread for the audition. I pronounced myself DOA and never entered the room. Gluten may destroy my body, but even Superman has his Kryptonite. Like the Man of Steel, I choose to fly anyway.

I wouldn't risk my health for an acting job, but I have taken other risks. In 2015, I made a particularly bold move; I walked away from my steady day job of five years because it no longer aligned with my dream of acting. I quit without having another job lined up. My health insurance flew out the window. I had no idea where my next paycheck would come from. I didn't care. I just had to get out. The known had become scarier than the unknown.

There's a Zen saying, *Leap and the net will appear.* When

I left that job, boy did I leap . . . right into a depression. Yes, I needed out, but I had also taken the leap to send a message to the universe that I was "all in" with acting. I had cleared my days for more auditions to come.

They didn't.

I had resigned from a fairly cushy job to support my acting career, and I'll be damned, it didn't support me back. I felt betrayed. *And where was this so-called net anyway?* It could not appear fast enough.

Fourteen years into this journey, and it was the first time my brain seriously considered choosing a different path. Luckily, my heart has a mind of its own.

As it turned out, the net was waiting for me in 2016. I started making more money with less hours at a new job with greater flexibility. Things started clicking with my new commercial agent, and my auditions skyrocketed. I lost count of how many commercials I booked that year! I also scored an audition for a supporting role in a feature film called *The Pinch*. Better yet, I booked it!

At the end of 2018, *The Pinch* was released on Amazon Prime. Watching myself as Gina, the mob wife, in a movie on Amazon Prime? Let's just say I had to pinch myself.

Each booking helps keep me in the game, yet I never know when the next one is coming. I've weathered 18 years of unpredictability. Sure, this can be unsettling, but I like the adventure of not knowing what's going to happen next. Being consumed with "next," on the other hand, presents its own challenges.

Suddenly, I'm beating myself up for not being where I want to be in my career, or maybe more appropriately,

where I think I *should* be. I'm focusing on everything I
haven't accomplished yet. I'm not a famous movie star. I
don't have my own television show. I haven't won an Oscar
or an Emmy.

But I have *won*. I'd be doing myself a serious disservice
if I didn't acknowledge how far I've come, if I didn't
downright celebrate my victories along the way. And if
I've won once, well, lightning can strike twice. I moved
to Hollywood to become an actress, and you know what?
I did what I said I was going to do! I have an agent. I
audition a lot. I've been on TV. People contact me to tell me
they've seen my commercials. I'm in a movie on Amazon
Prime. Just whose idea of success am I measuring myself
up against anyway?

I had to learn that success is a choice. It's a state of
mind. If you believe success is a future event, then you're
never successful. If you believe success is reserved for other
people, then you're never successful. No matter what you
believe, the show must go on. Whether you're starring in it
or not is completely up to you.

In the wise words quoted by the great philosopher, Ice
Cube, "Check yourself before you wreck yourself."

Recently while I was driving around Hollywood, I saw
a billboard with two famous actresses promoting their new
movie. I thought, "That must be kind of weird to see your
face on a billboard." Um . . . you know who else's face has
been on a billboard? Mine! Granted, it was in Fresno, but I
have pictures of it, and I've seen it with my own eyes along
the freeway. The billboard promotes a local casino, and the
tagline reads, *This is Winning.*

I am literally the face of winning! Anne Hathaway and Rebel Wilson ain't got nothing on me!

Ironically, booking an acting job is a lot like hitting the jackpot. Despite seemingly insurmountable odds, the certainty of *no* certainty, and the constant rejection, I'm still here after 18 years. I think I can safely say I've been nothing if not persistent. Illness, sacrifice, frustration, disappointment, self-doubt, fear, exhaustion, credit card debt, and long stretches of having nothing to show for my efforts haven't stopped me. I've stayed the course even in those times when it seemed like quitting was my only option.

That's the thing about quitting; it is *always* an option. It's also the only sure-fire way to lose.

I don't know what the future holds, but if I had to guess …you'll see me on a billboard with Tom Cruise promoting *Mission Impossible XXVII*. We take home Best Actor and Best Actress Oscars for the film, and we celebrate our wins by eating Kraft Macaroni & Cheese and Twinkies because celiac disease has been cured.

Anything can happen.

Biography

Candice Bolek is a Los Angeles-based actress who has enjoyed work in commercials, television, independent films, web series, and print. Candice grew up dancing competitively, making her love of performing and being on stage the perfect foundation for a career on camera. She has also written and produced her own content.

Candice Bolek

Candice graduated magna cum laude from Penn State University with a B.A. in Speech Communication and minors in Theatre and Business. Following college, she accepted a job at CBS in Detroit scheduling commercials, but her desire to act in them led her to Los Angeles. She is most often cast as "Mom" in commercials. As a result, she loves having husbands and kids all over Los Angeles.

Her stage presence and natural speaking ability have also served her well in the sales arena, where her presentations have caught the attention of other successful and in-demand speakers.

Candice has yet to meet Tom Cruise.

Contact Information

Email: candice.bolek@gmail.com
Instagram: @candicebolek
LinkedIn: Candice Bolek
IMDB: www.imdb.me/candicebolek

CHAPTER NINE

Find Your Better Life

Raynaldo Alexander

The unknown can be a fearful place, no matter how much faith you have. I say this from experience. When I was 26 with the body of a professional athlete and the faith of an unmovable boulder, kidney failure almost killed me.

A Marine veteran, I was a firefighter, a perfect physical specimen, and training to compete in firefighter competitions. My life turned upside down when I received the most devastating news of my life: My kidneys were so dysfunctional from massive scarring that my kidney function was at only about ten percent.

"There must be some type of mistake because I feel great!" I managed to tell the physician. My heart was pounding in fear.

"I'm sorry, but we will need to prepare you for dialysis soon," he said.

I remember sitting in his office in a zombie-like state, tears rolling down my face, shaking, thoughts screaming in my brain: *How can this happen? How can I provide for my wife and children? I won't be there to see my daughters graduate or get married! I live a good life; work, church, and back home. God, why are you giving me a death sentence so early? I'm not ready to die!*

I was devastated. In one moment, my faith, all the faith I'd *thought* I had, simply vanished. All that was left was fear.

The more I pushed myself past my limitations, the better I felt about myself.

As I slowly began to experience the effects of end-stage kidney failure, I had to leave my job. I developed gout; my feet would swell and hurt with a throbbing pain as though they were always angry with me. My kidneys were not filtering the toxins from my body. My body started to be very sluggish and my energy level reached an all-time low. I threw up constantly and violently until there was absolutely nothing left in my body. I would sit on the floor with my face inside the toilet, crying, asking God *Why?*

After I'd left my job, I bought a mower and lawn equipment because I knew I had to continue to provide for my family. I borrowed a trailer, found a rent-to-own car lot, and purchased an old truck. As a man, my job was to be the priest, provider, and protector; I was willing to die for that cause. The Louisiana summer heat—sometimes 103 degrees with 100% humidity—almost did kill me as I mowed yards and trimmed weeds.

By the time I started dialysis, I was terribly depressed and wanted to die. About three weeks into dialysis, my wife walked out. She said she was unhappy and though she loved me, she wasn't *in love* with me.

Whatever your current condition or circumstances, don't stop moving forward.

Our relationship had always been difficult. We were two young people from broken homes who didn't know the first thing about building a good marriage, but I still wanted her with me. I was broken, I was tired, I was lonely, and I was scared. She was the only person who had ever seen me break down and then she was gone. My emotions swung from hurt to anger, and all I could think was that I'd lost my life partner and my youngest daughter.

My wife's departure took the fight out of me. I distanced myself from everyone. I stopped calling friends, visiting my family, and attending church. I felt as though no one could possibly understand how I felt. And if I had not suffered enough, soon I lost every possession I owned in a house fire.

I moved into a small room in my aunt and uncle's house. My depression deepened, and I frequently thought of ending my life. One day after dialysis, my blood pressure dropped and I fainted, falling like a rock. When I opened my eyes to find myself face down on the floor, I cried silently, *I cannot live like this.*

I was humiliated and mortified. I always had been a leader, the strong one, the one other people needed and depended on, and had never felt weak before, emotionally or physically. I gained about 30 pounds and locked myself away in my small, borrowed room.

I was dying from the inside out.

One day, my two-year-old daughter hugged me and kissed me on the cheek as though she sensed my miserable state and wanted to comfort me. I began to sob painfully, crying so hard my head pounded, my eyes swelled, and I could not catch my breath. I cried, *God, you must help me, because if you don't, I'm going to die.*

Later when I was calm, I thought how my children would be affected if I left their lives, and I realized I had already left mentally and spiritually even though my battered body was still present. The realization made me sick to my stomach. I made a promise to myself: Before I die, I am going to *live!* And I was going to live in peace and prosperity.

Faith and fear can dwell side-by-side in your life when you're young, but it's impossible for them to coexist for very long. *Pursued faith* is a physical act of belief; it causes a supernatural boomerang effect that extends beyond your obstacle, circles back, hits it from behind and knocks it on its face.

The bible story about David, a young boy who faced the giant Goliath, is a beautiful example of faith. David sank a rock into the giant's forehead with a simple slingshot, knocking him down onto his face. When you pursue what you truly believe without fear of the obstacles in front of you, your act of faith knocks down whatever was standing before you.

I resumed my workouts, and the most profound thing happened: The more I pushed myself past my limitations, the better I felt about myself. I set up a challenging regimen, and each day I went to the gym before my morning dialysis and again in the evening.

The stronger my body got, the stronger I became spiritually and emotionally. The gym had become my sanctuary. Weighing 175 pounds and with a dialysis port hanging from my check, I bench pressed 315 pounds. A crowd gathered around me to watch me do dips with three 45-pound plates hanging from the belt around my waist. People at the gym were totally amazed and could not believe I was a dialysis patient. I began training family and friends in my morning sessions and started a bootcamp in the evenings. My clients named my bootcamp *Body-By-Ray*; we later changed the name to *Steel-Built Bodyz*.

As many as twenty clients at a time attended my ninety-day transformation camps, and their results were life-changing. They experienced the same transformations I had experienced—physical, spiritual, and emotional. My struggles had inspired each of them to give their all, and it created a special bond among us. They often told me I was their inspiration, yet they were *my* motivation as well.

One of my most faithful and hardworking clients was the dialysis clinical nurse who oversaw the entire business. I was her patient on Monday, Wednesday, and Friday mornings, and she was my bootcamp client on Monday through Friday evenings.

The most encouraging part of my journey is that when I finally decided to fight my circumstances and rediscovered my will to live, I inspired people to find their desire to live as well. Many times, I would finish my four-hour dialysis treatment and then sit next to another patient while I encouraged them to hang in there and be strong.

I started to feel as if the very thing that almost killed me became the very thing that built me. In the middle of chaotic situations are hidden life-building jewels and heart-piercing events which build you in ways not possible otherwise. I would never wish the things I experienced upon my enemies, yet now I wouldn't change a single thing that's happened to me. My trials made me what I am now.

People began to contact me to speak at schools, churches, and other places and events as well. I became the president of the Parent-Teacher Organization for two schools, simultaneously. I worked tirelessly with principals, teachers, parents, and students alike, and raised parental involvement dramatically. I began to coach community league flag football teams as well as tackle football teams for a Christian academy.

Very slowly, I slowly gravitated into mentoring parents and students, encouraging them to never give up. Any place I could help, any one I could inspire, I was there. I felt I had something to offer, and wanted to empower whomever I encountered to never give up. People began to forget that I was on dialysis. Everything and everyone I connected with seemed to improve.

My mindset about my own situation stabilized, and I came to this realization: If I receive a kidney transplant, fine. If I don't receive a transplant, that will be fine, too. No matter what happens, I choose to live and to live prosperously.

You can be as strong as steel, as solid as a granite block, tough as the toughest nail, and as great a fighter as all the famous contenders combined, but eventually you get tired of the battles and stop having the same fight in you that you once did. When you reach the point where you no longer have the drive to fight for yourself, you need to think about everyone who is depending on you to fight for them. My trigger was my children. Somewhere you will find your own trigger for your will to survive and push.

Though life can seem unfair, you need to know that the trials and tribulations you suffer have a purpose: They create your unique identity. You are unlike any other person. Things may affect you differently than they do anyone else; your one-of-a-kind blueprint can't be copied. You were created to walk on top of whatever tries to walk on you.

In August 2014, I received a call. The phone rang late at night and I recognized the area code as Iowa City, Iowa. I answered very cautiously and low, for I knew there could only be one reason to receive a call in the middle of the night from Iowa.

"Hello?"

"Mr. Alexander, are you ready?"

"Yes. Is this it? Is this *the call*?"

"Yes, this is *the call*," the nurse said, and then she gave me a long list of instructions.

When we ended the call, I spent a few minutes screaming, yelling, and crying, *Thank-you God!* My faith was raised to a level that was unimaginable. Then I looked at the time on my phone and realized it was 12:01 a.m.

"It's my birthday!" I yelled. "It's my birthday! I'm getting a kidney on my birthday!"

People read my Facebook posts and testify how my life has inspired, encouraged, and empowered them in so many ways.

It was the greatest moment of my life. I began to cry again, thinking of all my friends who died waiting for kidney transplants.

Through God's grace, I received that transplant on my birthday. My life has not been the same since. I go through life totally confident that great things can happen to people who are experiencing great hardships, as long as they just do not give up.

Since my transplant, I do my best to imprint my mark on all I can influence—the mark of hope and perseverance, the assurance to never give up.

People read my Facebook posts and testify how my life has inspired, encouraged, and empowered them in so many ways. I receive comments from strangers telling me that the posts about my life have given them hope at a point when they were contemplating suicide. I act as a life coach to several men with kidney problems right now. I make time to hear them and to help because I know how it feels, and I *never* want anyone to feel like I did.

To live life with no hope is to be physically alive but spiritually and emotionally dead. It's a horrible way to live. I often think, what if I had given up back then? What would have happened to the many people who I have influenced and helped along the struggle of my journey?

You must be more resilient than your challenges and your struggles. You *must* outlast them, you *must* outperform them, you *must* outwork them, and you *must* persevere with the mindset that at whatever cost, you will be the last person standing.

Whatever your current condition or circumstances, don't stop moving forward. If you continue to move forward, even at a creep, you eventually move past your obstacles faster than if you just stop in the middle of your misery. I am a firm believer that things won't always be the way they are. Your pain has the potential and the possibilities to push you into your next level. As it stands now, your life is an unfinished portrait and the finished picture has yet to be glimpsed.

When I decided to believe in myself, get off my do-nothing and start doing-something, it wasn't easy, yet I found my will to survive and pushed past my limitations.

You must develop a bulldog mentality and grab hold of what you're believing and striving for and don't let go! Your situational change is just the flip side of wanting to quit. You are the result of what you have accepted during your life. You can't control the hand you are dealt, but you are in control of how you play it.

Once I decided to fight for my life and for the life of my children, I was on the flip side of wanting to give-up. I knew I could never give up. Perseverance doesn't even start until after you become sick and tired of being sick and tired—that's when you must continue doing the right thing. When you reach that point, you've endured too much to just quit. Your payoff is closer than you think.

My life has completely turned around since I started my fight, and I encourage and empower people all around the world. Since I decided not to quit life, I have been blessed with such a rich, fulfilling existence, one I could never have imagined earlier.

Your new life is waiting for you.

Biography

Raynaldo Alexander is a dynamic motivational speaker, published author, life-coach, youth mentor, and certified personal trainer. He continues to empower people around the world with his message of perseverance and faith injecting hope into the minds, hearts, and souls of countless people around the world.

Raynaldo Alexander

He has been a tool of inspiration and empowerment in churches, prisons, youth conferences, men and women's events, and schools. His energy and ability to capture the attention of his audience, through his heartfelt story of facing the challenges of depression during years of dialysis at an early age to changing the lives of people on dialysis and inspiring people of all walks of life has been a blessing to thousands.

Raynaldo is the founder of Encouraged By Ray, which is a world renown business of counsel, guidance, and motivation. He attended Northwestern State University in Natchitoches with studies in Criminal Justice and Sociology. He also attended LSU Shreveport, studying Community Health concentrating on Physical Fitness. Raynaldo followed up with his fitness journey by attending Body Design University in Atlanta, Georgia, and finishing his internship at Body Design Personal Training, also in Atlanta, where he earned his Personal Training certification.

Raynaldo has collaborated with Johnny Wimbrey, Nik Halik, Les Brown, and many other profound authors around the world. His first book, *Break Through Featuring Raynaldo Alexander* sold out its first printing in just three weeks.

Raynaldo is also a U.S. Marine veteran, a trained firefighter, a professional commercial vehicle driver, and a lineman.

The greatest of all his accomplishments is being a father to his children. He has two daughters, Dayjah and Amariah, and two sons, Bryce and Raynaldo II.

Raynaldo is from Mansfield, Louisiana, but now resides in Mississippi. He plans on relocating to Louisiana or Texas to continue to inspire people through his personal boot-camp and fitness studio, Steel Built Bodyz.

Contact information

Email: ecouragedbyray.@gmail.com
Website: www.encouragedbyray.com
Facebook: encouragedbyray
Facebook: RaysBootCamp
Instagram: @encouragedbyray
Twitter: @encouragedbyray

CHAPTER TEN

Perfect Timing for Landing

Milos Kovac

I had just finished yet another practice flight during my private pilot training, and my instructor said, "You know what, I'm going to ask another instructor to have a few flights with you. You know what you need to do, but for some reason you're not doing it. I think you may benefit from hearing someone else's explanation."

Three months earlier after a successful second check ride, the same instructor had said, "Congratulation, Milos, on your successful flight. We need just a few more flights, maybe three weeks, and you'll be ready for the final exam."

He was probably frustrated by the almost-zero progress during the last three months of my training. I was frustrated, too. Only one item on my training remained, and I was not able master it: crosswind landings. I knew exactly what to do, was able to describe the maneuvers, but the exact timing and intensity of the corrections I needed to make were all over the place.

All my attempts to handle an airplane in crosswind landings were pure trial and error. The only thing I knew for sure was that my instructor didn't want to die so he would keep us alive even if I screwed up terribly.

What do we need to move into a flow state?
Be in love with what we do.

My internal trust in the skills of experts, whether it is a flight instructor or a coach, was born during my high school and university years. I did Taekwondo on an international level as a member of the Slovakian national team for several years. The martial arts are very physically and mentally demanding.

During those years, I built a close relationship with my coach. I did what he asked me to do the best way I could, without analyzing if it was doable. I was committed both mentally and physically, and I learned to trust his experience and assessment of the situation. That attitude led me to one of the biggest achievements in Slovakian Taekwondo international competition in that era.

During the summer of 1999, I was completely prepared for the upcoming season in my life. Physically and mentally, I was in the best shape ever. Our first international tournament was in Croatia. A few seconds into my first match, I was knocked out. It seemed as though it was a mild knockout; I remembered nothing, yet I wasn't visibly injured. The tournament was over for me, but the surprise came after the doctor's examination when he said, "No tournaments or hard workouts for the next six months."

After my six-month layoff, I was eager to start working, and I was willing to work hard and focus on getting in my best shape ever. But my coach had a different plan. He skipped the workout plan and signed me up for the next available tournament in Italy, one of the biggest we had participated in—he just told me, *You are ready*. And I listened to him.

To my surprise, I advanced to the final match quite easily. That final match was at a very high level, a much different level than any other at the tournament. It was an equal match for a long time because the techniques that got me to this point were not working well. Obviously, my competitor had studied my strategies very well and was prepared to overcome them.

My coach was watching my opponent closely as well. During a break before the last round he said, "As soon as he moves, use a different technique, not the one that you have been using so far." And he told me exactly which technique to use. When an opportunity came at the beginning of that final round, I scored. At that moment, I felt my competitor take a mental step back. I won the entire tournament; it was one of the biggest achievements in Slovakian Taekwondo. Definitely, it was the biggest moment for me. My martial arts experience built my trust in my coach to an extremely positive level. In 2014, about 15 years later, it was a time to use trust again.

I had already completed way more flight hours than the average pilot for flight school, flying at least twice per week. Time was running out quickly, and so was the available balance on my credit card. An additional challenge was the fast-approaching date of my departure from the United States to France. I knew that if I didn't finish my training in the United States, it would be far more challenging to do so in France.

The second instructor was not very successful in helping me with a breakthrough, either, so after four flights, I returned to my primary instructor.

Some of my crosswind landings were okay, but some of them most certainly would have been off the runway if I had not interrupted my landing. I couldn't count how many times I hit the ground with my wheels not facing the direction we were headed. I even landed sideways, and the tires probably were visibly smoking. My instructor often told me not to worry, as the landing gear was very strong.

Almost two months later, just two weeks before my departure to France, I was on an approach for landing with decent crosswind. It was an ideal situation for training. Just before touchdown, I did the required correction. It was a little bit too soon, as usual, but this time it felt different. I felt some small, but recognizable response of the airplane. After almost five months of training on crosswind landings, this was my first breakthrough.

We circled around the airport and the next landing was with an almost perfect correction. I felt the airplane's response when I moved the controls for rudder and aileron.

It is hard to explain this difference, but I'll try. Imagine a sweet taste in your mouth, as if you had been fed a spoonful of honey. And then imagine it again, but this time the spoon's really in your mouth. And imagine it again, but you're actually swallowing the honey. It's a huge difference.

From that moment I knew exactly what I did right and wrong during landing. I then focused on fine-tuning my landing skills, and successfully completed my final check ride just two days before I left the country for France.

So, what was happening during these five long months of pilot training? I had clearly defined a goal. It was *my* goal and I really wanted to make it happen. On the conscious level, I knew exactly what to do. Since this information had not reached my subconscious level yet, my body was not able to feel the plane and make the corrections necessary to keep it under control in the tricky crosswind landings.

Yet, I kept my attention and focus on my goal and practiced it again and again. Yes, it was frustrating, but the decision to quit was not an option. Nothing was wrong with me, the airplane, or my instructor. I fully trusted that my instructor knew what he was doing.

I was doing my best to keep my consciousness, emotions, and body in harmony. But the alignment was not visible for a long time. With persistence and repetition, my old paradigm shifted to a new one. I was able to feel on the conscious level a response of the airplane to my tiny control movement. From that point everything went really fast to a successful end. It took almost double the number of flight hours that are the average for private pilot training, but I made it.

My frustration went down during those last two weeks; I was more relaxed. That allowed me to understand air traffic control patter more easily and monitor much more information from the avionics on my displays.

You can imagine something similar if you compare your skill levels between your teenage driving lessons and your driving today. Now you can tune your radio, talk with somebody else, watch your kids, and monitor a huge amount of car traffic flowing around you in different directions as you competently steer, brake, and accelerate. If you'd attempted this workload during your first few drives with an instructor, everybody in your path would have been in danger.

What happened to me during my last two weeks of flight school? I was able to get into a flow state, a state of mind where thoughts, feelings, and actions are in harmony. When we're in a flow state, we're not paying attention to anything else, just to what we are doing. We get pleasure from the activity itself, not thinking about what happened before, or what will be after we are done with it. This is a state of mind with extreme effectivity and productivity.

It is an optimal state of consciousness where we feel and perform our absolute best. We do not think about "what if" questions. We do not prepare backup plans. We do not analyze if somebody may perceive us as ridiculous in that moment. We do not judge anybody, or anything. We are not frustrated by the lack of time to solve this task on schedule, or that you would be happier to do something else.

There is no good or bad, there is just now.

What do we need to move into a flow state? *Be in love with what we do.* We need to feel included in that activity, to feel it's important to us and we are important for it.

We need to do just a single task and be focused on it in that moment. Then we can do our tasks much faster, much better, and solve problems that somebody else may consider impossible to solve.

It's like using a magnifying glass to spark a fire. We don't need more sunlight; instead, we need to focus the light we already have to one intense point. Flow states are similar. They are moments of rapt attention when we get so focused on the task at hand that everything else disappears and all aspects of our performance go through the roof.

I believe these abilities are inherent, that everyone has them. I've often seen my kids in a flow state. Their imaginations and ability to visualize are so strong they can turn off the world around them and build a new one in their mind. At that moment, they are truly in love with what they are doing, often even having emotional reactions.

Our subconscious mind cannot differentiate between what is real and what is not. Do you remember how many times you have had goose bumps or even cried when you were watching a movie? The scene wasn't real, yet it had a real physical effect on you. Why? Because you were emotionally connected with the movie, you allowed information from the outside world to pass through your conscious mind down to your subconscious mind.

Kids are able to build such a world directly in their imagination, and they don't need external input. Sometimes it is very difficult to get them out of that world if we need to. They are in a flow state and we force them to leave it, to do "mandatory" activities even though the kids don't want to. We teach them to live our lifestyle, use our way of thinking, and we program them to be little replicas of ourselves. Sooner or later children lose the abilities that might help them to build a much better life than we have.

I really believe that computers bring various opportunities to our kids and I support them with whatever they ask for, with only one condition: I want them to *create* something. Almost two years ago, my nine-year-old son showed me a virtual machine he created, but it failed to work several times during his demo. He was not happy, and so he dived even deeper into his work, trying to solve some technical problems.

On a Friday evening, he told me that he needed to work on his computer on Saturday and Sunday so he could finish his project and show me how it ran. I let him spend the entire weekend on the computer, and he really focused on creating something new.

On Sunday evening, he invited my wife and me to see the new virtual machine he created, a type of rocket that he built as part of a machine-building game called Scrap Mechanic. It was working—well, it was doing something. He was trying hard to explain to us how it worked, but I did not follow his thoughts. After focusing more on his explanation, I understood, and I was thrilled. Whatever he was saying to me, it seemed he had somehow added mathematical operations into his machine.

After further discussion, I really understood what he was doing. Binary mathematical operations were a challenge that he had been working on for a while, something that he hadn't learned yet and wouldn't study at school for at least four or five years.

I asked him how and where he had learned the mathematical process. He explained he had seen a similar machine on some internet videos, and tried to replicate it in his game, but it didn't work well. So, he decided to learn how the system worked and searched out educational videos on the internet and learned those principles.

I was a proud dad. It took me a while to understand his language and his explanation about how binary operations work. With persistence and dedication, he studied on his own and solved his problem without help from me. I asked him why he never asked for help. He answered it was supposed to be a surprise, so he wanted to do it on his own.

This is an example why I believe that with persistence, self-discipline, and desire to work on the task at hand, we can solve any problem and learn whatever we need to learn right in time, when we need it. Our kids are masters of that ability, so let them teach us *their* way of learning.

I believe children are able to broaden and retain their abilities. Just imagine the advancement of our civilization once this happens. My vision is to build community centers as alternatives to the current education system, where every kid will have access to the resources required to get real experience of everything they have learned through traveling, by using the latest technologies and access to the best professionals in every area of our lives.

Through coaching individuals and businesses to understand their potential and shift individual and group paradigms, I show them how they can achieve their goals and inspire others.

I invite you to join me so we can work together and be an example of inspiration for the next generation.

Biography

Milos Kovac, his wife, Maria, and their children, Milos and Marko, have lived in Slovakia, the United States, France, and now the Czech Republic.

As a human potential explorer, he exposes parents to their kids' potential and empowers them to live a family lifestyle full of fun, self-development, freedom, and fulfillment. His life mission is to

Milos Kovac

advance kids' education to the next level, where every child will fully comprehend and appreciate their unique abilities. Milos believes that elementary education should be about discovering yourself, and learning how to develop your intellect and set up and achieve goals.

Contact information

Email: milos@miloskovac.org
Website: www.miloskovac.org

CHAPTER ELEVEN

Live Outside the Lines

Sonia Wysingle

Someone's opinion of you does not
have to become your reality.
—**Les Brown**

According to the naysayers, I'm not supposed to be here. I should be in a hopeless place where I am torn, broken, and living a life full of trauma and despair. Naysayers will tell you I'm supposed to be helplessly dependent upon others, looking to them for my survival. With the help of statistics, they'll declare that an individual with my beginnings surely can't make it to the level where I stand now, and certainly can't do the things that I'm doing.

Born as the fifth of six children to a single mother and an absent father in a small town with few opportunities to enhance my quality of life, I was presumed to be destined for nothing great.

According to the naysayers, I'm better off being one of the forgotten ones—those who are muted, invisible, left out, helpless, powerless, fearful, and ashamed. According to some statistics, my net worth is equated to the reduced value of a $5 bill.

It's pointless to point your finger to blame others because it doesn't change what has happened.

If the naysayers were to forecast my story starting with my birth, I am supposed to be struggling, angry, unintelligible, and uncouth. The statistics and probabilities all point to a life of being below average, lacking confidence, ambition, and accomplishments, filled with limitations and brokenness.

Well, I'm so very glad the naysayers were never friends of mine. I'm relieved to know the statistical reports have failed at every turn to reflect the facts of my individuality.

One of my favorite wise men and orators, Les Brown, has shared something profound, a piece of wisdom I feel is so true about the naysayers and the negative statistical reports about my life's direction. When he was a young boy, one of Les' peers voiced a derogatory remark about him. His math teacher overheard and reassured Les, "Someone's opinion of you does not have to become your reality."

What a phenomenal perspective! Those words have the potential to breathe life into a dismal spirit. Those few words spoken by his math teacher caused Les Brown's world to shift. I believe those words contributed to the trajectory of his life and helped launch him into the great man he is today.

If you were to ask people who actually know me to share facts about me, they would probably say many different things. You would hear, *she's a proud Navy veteran, a great and wise teacher,* and *a tremendous coach.*

You would also hear that I am a silver medalist, very understanding, patient, full of humor, and witty. You'd hear that I am quite ambitious, innovative, very inspiring, and one who loves to elevate those around her.

Each description's common denominator would be that I am a successful person. I agree with those descriptions. I believe they are absolutely true. I am those things and much more. I am blessed and fulfilled and pleased with the person I have become. I can say with assurance that I have accomplished a great deal and I am looking forward to an even more notable future.

I believe we can have, be, and accomplish whatever we desire. There is no limit to the greatest, highest, and truest expression of ourselves. We are a creation of progression and abounding love. I understand we each have a purpose. We all have a path to travel and a journey to complete. How we travel along our path and walk through our journey is really up to us. What we must do is remain focused and truly believe so we can become whatever our heart desires.

From Fatherless to Fulfilled

Growing up as a child without a father, I felt abandoned and rejected, and I often fluctuated between feelings of inadequacy and disappointment. Unable to communicate my hopelessness with my mother, I turned to basketball. The sport immediately and seamlessly became my father, friend, and teacher.

My love of the game taught me some very valuable lessons. Basketball taught me how to persevere and be disciplined, loyal, committed, and humble. The one thing that it did *not* teach me was how to deal with the void I so desperately wanted my father to fill.

Little did I know that one day I would have the opportunity to discover that my father had always been in my life, just under a different role. It's amazing how God works when you set your intention and never waiver in your truth.

Forgive and Forget

When I was 31, I learned my godfather was actually my biological father. I went for years not knowing that this man, my godfather, who would pick me up on weekends to spend time with him and his daughters, was *actually* my father. That meant my friends, whom I called *godsisters,* were *actually* my sisters. When I received that information from the person who loved me the most, I was overwhelmed with mixed feelings of being found, robbed, truly loved, and betrayed all at once.

I experienced so many intersecting and conflicting

emotions when I learned the truth about my father, I knew I had to quickly create a system to organize my thoughts. Over the next few weeks, I created a virtual filing system in my heart where I unpacked the details of each emotional impact. At the end of this healing process, after I'd sorted out all my emotions, I found one inconspicuous folder hidden underneath all those files. This one file was the folder of forgiveness, and it was key in allowing me to find purpose, contentment, and clarity in who I truly was.

I opened the folder of forgiveness and it allowed me to begin the process of forgetting and healing. I learned I had to forgive the one whom I knew loved me the most. I had to wholeheartedly forgive my mother for protecting me from the validation for which I had blindly searched for— for so many years.

For my entire life I'd believed something that was not true. As a young girl trying to solve the mystery of my situation with my infinite imagination with finite imagination, I'd believed my father left my mom because she gave birth to a girl. I was sure I was never wanted because I was not what he expected.

Years later, I learned his decision to leave had nothing to do with me. He was gone long before my mother knew she was pregnant.

The valuable lesson I learned is that people make decisions based on where they are at the moment, and for a variety of reasons I might not even imagine. Most individuals would make different decisions if they had it to do over. My mom allowed me to continue with the thought that I had a godfather and never really mentioned anything about my father. I realized she never shared anything about my father when I was a child because she felt I couldn't possibly understand.

From this experience, I learned it's pointless to point your finger to blame others because it doesn't change what has happened. Forgiveness is a precious decision that frees all involved. When you can forgive others for their offenses and forget the deed by releasing every emotional tie connected to the person or offense, then that's the essence of true forgiveness and forgetting.

Permission to be Great

As a young woman, I didn't realize how deeply my earlier years had affected me and how they continued to influence my behavior and decisions. I was a late bloomer. Instead of using my 20s to explore and allow my experiences to mold me into the woman I was to become, I spent the better part of my time avoiding things that could have led to possible rejection and failure. I allowed the dismal feelings of rejection and abandonment that were still festering in me from my childhood to dictate the narrative of my life for far too long.

My actions were dreary and predictable. I always settled for the next best thing, I treated fear as though it was real, and I deferred to others far too often. I preferred to shrink and become invisible in a crowd rather than bring attention to my presence. Somewhere along the way, I taught myself that dimming my light wards off the risk of rejection. The logical result was I considered myself inadequate, small, unimportant, and unworthy of the very best.

YOU ARE WORTHY

Fortunately for me, I finally reached a point where I grew tired of being invisible to the world. It wasn't until I was wallowing in self-pity, sitting on the floor in my bathroom staring down the face of a life-altering and permanent decision, that I discovered the earth-shaking truth that changed my life. In that moment, I learned that I *truly* mattered. Even more important, I learned to *whom* I mattered and *why*: I mattered to *me*, and this was more than enough. This meant everything to me because I am blessed with a gift to heal the hearts of the abandoned and rejected. I am meant to help those who are confused and lost discover a new day and find the designated path.

All these years later, I still clearly remember the moment when I learned I truly mattered. Though a few thoughts were forming and floating in my mind, one concept really got my full attention. I remember clearly hearing these words, in this exact order: *A thing is only as important as you make it.*

Throughout my younger years and up to that point of reflection, I never considered myself important. Never did I truly feel within my core that I was important. I allowed my feelings of abandonment to lead me into believing I wasn't good enough, that I was unworthy of greatness.

LIVING IN YOUR PURPOSE WITH CLARITY

Because I finally chose to heal the wounds left by rejection and abandonment, I have realized my life's purpose. I am clear about what it takes to live a satisfying, productive life while fulfilling my purpose.

Although I can't recall the exact day or time when I realized my life's purpose with absolute clarity, I do remember everything about how I felt. I recall intense feelings of determination, commitment, and excitement. I felt like I had *finally* discovered the most important answer as to why I existed.

And *you* are at the center of it all.

I discovered that my purpose in life, and the gift with which the Creator has blessed me, was never for me—it was for each of you who can benefit and be blessed by what I have to offer. You see, that day I realized with absolutely clarity that my gift was not for me. My gift is to heal hearts and help people understand they are not alone. My gift is to tell the broken-hearted they are not forgotten, they do matter, and they have always been good enough. My gift has allowed me to create a number of systems and quality programs that can move a willing and committed person from broken to confident, from rejected to fulfilled, and from lost to leading.

I can do this because I comprehend that everything in our reality originated in the one place most individuals fail to look. That single place is the absolute reason why each of us either has what we have, or we don't! Period. We are creators and we create from this realm every single day, twenty-four hours a day, seven days a week. I have been so blessed to truly understand how the mind allows and disallows occurrences in our lives and how things show up in our everyday lives.

This all solely depends on the manner in which we create.

EMPOWER YOU

I have been blessed with the understanding that we are our own most valuable strategist. We are *truly* empowered from a deep-seated realm that is responsible for governing our lives. The only lasting and sure way to remain inspired, motivated, and empowered comes from the programming of that particular system within the mind. To be completely empowered as the being you were created to be and live in your purpose with clarity, there are certain things you must understand and know assuredly. You must understand *you*. And in order to understand *you*, you must pay very close attention to every nuance and detail of your being.

To share a bit from one of the systems I designed, I will tell you that you must be willing to be completely honest with yourself. To begin the journey toward empowerment, we must be willing to peel back the layers of who we understand ourselves to be, to get to the core of why we are who we are, and why we do the things we do.

I am so pleased to have the opportunity to share with you and to love on you through my words. My desire for you is for you to become the loving creation you were designed to be, and to know that you have always been good enough. Greatness dwells on the inside of you; only you can unleash the power of your being and enrich the lives of others in the way that only *you* can.

Be well.

Biography

Sonia Wysingle

Sonia Wysingle is a transformational speaker, author, and teacher. Growing up as a fatherless child in a small town, Sonia discovered she could be exactly what she wanted to be, regardless of her beginnings in life. Sonia's global message transforms the hearts of those who have been rejected and abandoned, into individuals who embrace life with confidence, clarity, and persistence.

The author of three other books, Sonia is best known for *Fatherless Child: Healing Your Wounds of Rejection Doesn't Have to Scar Your Spirit.*

She resides in Little Elm, Texas, with her twin sons.

Contact Information:

Email: soniaswysingle@gmail.com
Website: soniawysingle.com
Booking: booksoniawysingle@gmail.com
Facebook: Sonia Wysingle
Twitter: @wysingle
Instagram: @SoniaWysingle

CHAPTER TWELVE

Persistence Brings Success

Jason Garrett

E verything changed the day the person closest to me in the whole world—my mother—was tragically taken away from my family. The person who wore so many hats for us and her coworkers, the person whom I credit with helping me with everything from work to relationships, was gone. I wondered if I could continue without her. I was lost and confused and I would have to go on.

Three other family members died in the same tragedy. All four were women, all the heads of their families. It was an event that devastated my entire extended family.

I remember what they had taught us, and a few points stand out:

- Walk by faith and not by sight.
- Continue to educate yourself throughout your life.
- Learn something daily.
- Keep your family together at all costs.

- Love others just as animals do—specifically, as dogs do. Canines don't care about race, color, or gender. They love unconditionally and completely. Responsibility for teaching obedience and friendliness rests completely with the owners, but overall, dogs learn to love on their own, with no human instruction involved.

Always be persistent and success will follow you on your path to greatness.

Those five great points *pushed* me to move on, keeping their memories alive in the way I lived my life moving forward. I carried the torch, hoping to make them proud.

Perhaps I survived because I backed out of the trip at the last minute. My mother and I had a great talk the day before the accident; we even joked about the rental car not being *up to par*, according to my great-aunt's standards, but the black Ford Fusion they'd rented would be a great gas-saver for them. I ensured she understood why I backed out from joining them. It was to be a trip for older—*seasoned*—women and I opted to pass.

That decision spared my life but led to more than two years of survivor's guilt.

It would be my job to educate others. No other family would have to go through what we went through. The accident could have been avoided, right? By eating better? Exercising? Taking medications?

The driver of the tractor-trailer that hit them did none of those things, so diabetes, in a sense, destroyed my family. I do believe this. The first two months after the accident were a blur to me—just a foggy memory. I stopped caring about things and my life seemed to happen without having a purpose. I started gaining weight. I wasn't exercising. There was no socializing. Relationship problems developed and added to the mix.

Trying to keep my extended family together while I was losing my immediate one was a tough task. Then it happened.

The Fire Department realized its members were dying too soon after retirement and we weren't as healthy as we should have been. To combat the problem, the Fire Administration created an awesome wellness program. Members started finding out about their existing medical problems and were able to start treatment immediately. The program would change our way of thinking and help us to lead healthier lives, thus giving firefighters a chance at longevity.

During my evaluation, I found out I had metabolic syndrome and was prediabetic. I was not shocked by the results, but I knew I could reverse it. I would personally find a nutrition program that would work for me and a counselor to deal with life after losing my loved ones. Finding my counselor, Brenda, started a three-year relationship that would help us both. She would encourage me to move forward, being very persistent and not allowing me to give up on my family and career. The news about my health was not a shock, but rather an eye-opener that would spearhead a movement to help others live a healthier life without medication.

My approach to obstacles is to jump in with both feet, so I hit this prediabetic thing hard. I would not say I liked talking about medicine, and the doctors didn't exactly give me the formula for success. After some research, I learned that metabolic syndrome is a cluster of problems: high blood pressure, high LDL (bad cholesterol) and low HDL (good cholesterol), high blood glucose (sugar), and belly fat.

Trying to keep my extended family together while I was losing my immediate one was a tough task.

There was a popular diet at the time called the *South Beach Diet*, and it would help me to improve my numbers within the first six weeks. Generally, the diet is higher in protein and healthy fats but lower in carbohydrates than an average eating plan. I even traveled to Miami Beach, Florida, to examine the culture that made the diet so famous and successful. To my surprise, the doctor who created the phenomenon was an amazing cardiologist. Arthur Agatston, who developed the diet, found that eating healthy will resolve many chronic health conditions.

Utilizing that formula of eating healthy, while not starting any form of physical fitness, I had *Pushed Until Success Happened.* It was a great feeling, and I knew that I could help others facing the same health issue.

It took about eight years of being *persistent* with my doctors to get them to utilize a different blood glucose test. I was not satisfied with the standard hemoglobin A1c test, which looks at blood sugar levels over a three-month period, because too many factors could influence the results; I took mine after admitting to not fasting the previous night. The nurse assured me the test would be accurate, but I wasn't happy with the results.

I looked for a more accurate test, because the A1c's no-fasting requirement puzzled me. I had never heard of that test before.

God gives us gifts, not for us, but to share with others.

My aggressive approach to health helped me reach a new, young, energetic doctor who worked with a veteran doctor who was well known for getting results. I'll call him Dr. P, and he was from a prominent hospital on the East Coast. My case intrigued him. Based on my bloodwork, I should have had type 2 diabetes, but I did not. Dr. P wanted to hear what I was doing. He asked me for my story.

"No disrespect," he said, "but I haven't seen much *success* from many people in your culture, how are you doing it?" We discussed the plan that I had created, my workouts and approach, and he did something very profound, and I thank God for his actions. He wanted to see what my pancreas was "actually doing" after meals. He did not want me to take the standard blood glucose test, but a test called the Oral Glucose Tolerance Test. I agreed.

This test takes about three hours. You are given a drink at the beginning of the procedure—something super-sweet like the Kool-Aid from National Lampoon's *Vacation*. The nurse tests your blood sugar every 30 minutes after administering the drink. What they are examining is how long it takes for the blood glucose numbers to drop. Mine was falling slower than they should have, which is normally not good.

What's wrong? It did not make any sense! After the last blood draw, I was completely exhausted, hungry, frustrated, and annoyed, and my right arm ached. Dr. P called me afterward to let me know everything was okay.

"I'm a phenom, right, doc?" I asked.

"Yes! Keep doing what you're doing, Mr. Garrett."

So now that I have the formula for success, what do I do with it?

God gives us gifts, not for us, but to share with others. Over the next year, I started to apply that system that I was using and enhance it for others. It would be a sustainable and reliable system using an acronym that I created: *The POISED Lifestyle.*

It's not labeled a diet because that word sounds so restrictive and intimidating—like a task, chore, or work. It is a lifestyle, as people in many other countries live. The Blue Zone is the region in the world where people live much longer and live with low rates of chronic disease. I had done a research paper on the *Mediterranean Diet* and was very intrigued. Many of these weight loss centers and fad diets (the *South Beach Diet* to name one) use that curriculum approach or a form of it.

The diets involve consuming mainly fresh fish and lean meats, whole fruits, and vegetables, and even allow for eating some dark chocolate and drinking red wine for dinner. It was a great strategy, and I would not only use this formula but live my life on it.

My clients—athletes, over-the-road truck drivers, doctors, nurses, business professionals, friends, and family members—have a 100% success rate.

Simplifying my meat consumption to only wild-caught fish will yield great results for me and solidify my strategy to approach the better quality of life and better health that I was hoping for. My quest was to help any and every person that I encountered with type 2 diabetes or prediabetes to get off medicine and sustain that. I decided to educate myself and become equipped with the appropriate tools for my toolbox to help others properly.

Four-year schools were not an option at this point in my life. So online courses, day and night courses, trips to various facilities, and life training were my routes. First becoming a Certified Personal Trainer and a Nutrition and Wellness Coach, then a Diabetes Lifestyle Coach and a member of the American Association of Diabetes Educators, and finally a Diabetes Educator and Community Health Worker for a healthcare system in Dallas, Texas.

My clients have had a 100% success rate. They include athletes, over-the-road truck drivers, doctors, nurses, business professionals, friends, and family members.

To whom much is given, much is required, Luke 12:48 (English Standard Version). Given the formula, much is required from me to help others.

My *persistence* also got the protein shake that I created on the menu in the Fuel Zone (Food and Shake Store) at Cowboys Fit Gym—located at the Dallas Cowboys Headquarters in Frisco, Texas. That came about after I purchased the ingredients myself and handed out samples at the gym to show how good it tasted and how it was an excellent post-workout alternative to food. My clients and other employees agreed, and eventually, management added the Blueberry Muffin shake to the gym menu. Once again, I had *Pushed Until Success Happened.*

As a child, I can remember asking my mother and sister for things. At times they would say no, but my persistence usually seemed to pay off in the end. Heck, I was a cute kid with an afro who loved to talk and was polite. Who could say no to that?

I can recall being interested in a young lady. She initially declined my requests that she accompany me on a date, but changed her mind after a couple of weeks. I asked her why she had a change of heart, and she told me it was because I had not given up on asking and had been very polite and understanding of her rejection. The relationship didn't work out, but being persistent secured that first date.

We should push ourselves as birds do. A bird knows it has to build a nest for its young—it's a non-negotiable requirement. Through good or bad weather, predators, and other obstacles, building that nest is a necessary task. They create the nest by moving one twig at a time, being very persistent until it's finished.

When the time comes, those baby birds must learn how to fly. It's something they've watched their parents do, but never tried for themselves. The first couple of attempts won't be perfect; perhaps the fledglings will even have a crash or two and some window-bumping. But don't worry, because of their *persistence,* success will happen—eventually!

Soon they're flying higher and higher each day, never remembering their earthbound days.

The same can be true of you.

Fly higher every day. Reach higher every day.

Always be persistent and success will follow you on your path to greatness.

Biography

Jason Garrett is a veteran of the U.S. Marine Corps and a retired firefighter. He's a certified personal trainer and wellness/nutrition coach in private practice with a focus on prediabetes. He also works as a diabetes educator for a large health care system in Dallas, Texas.

Jason Garrett

Jason has two children, Jason Alexander Garrett Jr., 20, and Kameron Alexandria Garrett, 12.

Jason has had 100 percent success rate in improving client health, appearance, and overall performance. Jason believes that a plant-based diet, physical fitness, stress reduction, and education can reverse all chronic diseases.

He is the author of *Not On My Watch: A Firefighter's Guide—Reversing Prediabetes Take Control Of Your Life.* The large-print edition was released May 10, 2019.

Jason is a member of Elevate Life Church, assisting on the Outreach Team, and a member of the American Association of Diabetes Educators where he is a facilitator for the National Diabetes Prevention Program.

Contact Information:

Email: thepoisedlifestyle@gmail.com
Website: www.poisedlifestyle.org
Instagram: @coachjasonagarrett

CHAPTER THIRTEEN

Keep Pushing Until You Succeed

Bernard Beausoleil

Some people are dealt a bad hand when starting out in life, yet they still do well. Is it the luck of the draw or is it destiny? Starting out in life with a good hand does not guarantee you success. We've all met educated derelicts. Conversely, some of the most successful people on the planet have overcome monumental, almost impossible obstacles and achieved huge success despite their immense struggle. They're truly inspirational people and role models.

I would say I was dealt a pretty good hand at the beginning of my life, being born in Scotland to a British mother and a career U.S. Air Force sergeant.

First, I was born a U.S. citizen with its obvious advantages and benefits, and my British mother gave me close, fun-loving British aunts, uncles, and cousins.

Second, growing up as an Air Force brat, our family moved every two to three years. Instead of moving from one street or town to another, we moved from one country to another. All seven of us children were forced to be very adaptable at an early age. We learned to get out of our shells, to get out of our comfort zones, and make new friends as soon as possible.

Third, because we met and lived among people of different cultures, races, and religious backgrounds, we did not grow up to be judgmental or racist.

Just when you think you are on your last straw, that is when you need to push a little bit more to achieve success!

Fourth, throughout my travels abroad and throughout the United States, I came to four conclusions:

1. Everyone has the same dreams, goals, aspirations, struggles, setbacks, failures, successes, good and bad habits, shortcomings, frustrations, money problems, hassles, traffic jams, etc.
2. Every parent wants their children to have a better life than they had.
3. Everyone is different, with different languages, customs, traditions, formalities, dress, rules, religions, slang expressions, political friends and foes, food, drink, sports, etc.
4. Everywhere you go, the road to success is always under construction.

In July 1967, my dad, Air Force Tech Sergeant Joseph "Frenchy" Beausoleil, was given his new set of orders to report to Detachment 3, 7350th Support Group, Tempelhof Air Base, West Berlin, Germany. Joan, my mom, grew up in Great Britain during World War II, was bombed by Germans, lost loved ones, and was strafed by a Messerschmitt ME-109 fighter when she was just 14 years old. An unknown heroic person grabbed her and threw her behind a rock wall as bullets riddled the wall.

When Mom found out we were going to be living among German people in Berlin, she went ballistic. Finally, Dad talked her into accepting the new adventure with the key selling point that she was close to England and could visit her family.

For five years, my family enjoyed great adventures and travel throughout West Berlin, West Germany, Bavaria, and Great Britain. As a bonus, I was selected to attend the Boy Scout World Jamboree in Mt. Fuji, Japan.

When we moved to West Berlin, my parents didn't ship much furniture from our home in Wisconsin due to military weight restrictions and the fact that our assigned three-story home in Berlin was fully furnished.

My parents loved European antiques, and they wanted to acquire some to ship stateside. On weekends, Mom and Dad went *Gelegenheiten,* which has a rough German to English translation of *bargain hunting for old antique-like furniture.* They discovered great bargains, often buying from a lawyer-turned-antique dealer named Uwe, who became a friend of the family.

Uwe became aware of my dad's pending retirement and his upcoming last duty assignment in Jacksonville, Florida. Uwe, a very ambitious young man, wanted to establish a retail or wholesale presence in America. Suddenly, our 1965 Chevy station wagon began coming home full to the brim with wooden furniture, hand-carved grandfather clocks, paintings, china, crystal, and bric-a-brac.

My dad worked out a consignment deal with Uwe: Upon his retirement in Florida, Dad would rent a small retail storefront, and Uwe would ship on consignment several 40-foot shipping containers loaded with West Berlin antiques. The plan called for our entire family to pitch in and work our butts off, sell the goods, and pay off Uwe as fast as possible. This would be our family's new source of income and—hopefully—my parents' retirement.

While in Berlin, our family cleaned entire apartments part-time for $65 per apartment, and the money went into savings. By 1972, through frugal living, careful spending, military discounts, benefits, and cleaning apartments, my parents saved $10,000. That was a lot of money back then.

By the summer of 1972, we regretfully left Berlin and arrived in Jacksonville. What had taken five years to save was spent and gone in a month, getting the store set up and paying the substantial freight invoices.

I attended Jacksonville University and worked part-time at WTLV-TV. When I was not in classes or working, I helped my parents sell antiques and art in their new store, getting hands-on business and sales experience.

After a year, I took a break from JU and went back to West Berlin. I had missed Berlin and was very depressed.

When we departed, I had kissed my girlfriend goodbye at the airport, boarded the plane, and never saw her again. It was not a good time for me. My close friends in West Berlin had been shipped out all over the world. I was starting over. I didn't like my life and I was not happy commuting 25 miles to JU. I felt disconnected from the college experience.

It was exciting to be back in Germany. I stayed for six adventurous months with Uwe and his wife Dorothy, working for room and board and getting valuable on-the-job training. I learned everything possible about exporting, packing, shipping, writing manifests, buying, selling, negotiating, and importing German antique furniture, art, and collectibles. I was 19 years old.

When Uwe told me that we would be meeting a prominent antique dealer/importer from California, I didn't realize what a huge impact it would have on me, my future success, and my future bank account. The importer was interested in buying a large number of hand-carved antique grandfather clocks. We drove over to meet him at a huge 100,000-square foot warehouse which was absolutely stuffed with thousands of them.

The American importer gave us a large order for clocks. I was fortunate to meet him and we quickly established a good rapport. I was curious how he could buy and sell such a large number of clocks and asked him how he did it. He pulled out a folded copy of a full-page ad he had placed in a major California newspaper, unfolded it, and told me what he had done. Then, he folded up the advertisement and put it away.

Though I never saw him again, I never forgot what he showed me. I decided that if I ever got the chance, I was going to do the same thing somewhere.

During my six-month stay in Berlin, I worked hard, six days a week, buying and selling antiques from estates, apartments, and homes, as well as packing and shipping 40-foot containers for export to the United States.

Just before I left West Berlin to return home, I ran into old friends, an Air Force captain and his wife. They invited me over for dinner and while catching up, asked me what I was doing back in Berlin. I described my work and the beautiful antique buffets and clocks and their great bargain prices. By the time we were done with dinner, they told me they wanted to buy an 1865 large carved walnut buffet sight unseen for 450 Deutsch marks, the equivalent of about $150.

I told Uwe about my sale and he was very pleased. He also told me he was impressed with my rapport with customers at his antique shop. He said he liked my work ethic and hustle, and said he wanted to set me up in business when I got back to the states.

After I returned from Berlin in 1973, I went to an antique show in Gadsden, Alabama, displayed and sold my parents' antiques. Fred, a family friend who restored chipped crystal glassware, joined me at the show. One morning at our Holiday Inn, Fred and I were getting ready to have breakfast, and he asked me if I had a good night's sleep.

"No, I didn't, because I had this incredible vision, more than a dream," I told him. "I was moving out west, and I had a very large warehouse with glass display windows on the front with angled stairs going up in front. There was a big showroom with a huge warehouse in the rear, with container doors up front and one in the rear."

Fred dismissed my vision.

When I returned to Florida from Alabama, Uwe visited us. He encouraged Dad to let me go to Dallas and open an import warehouse. After much discussion, Dad agreed and I went into business with his help. I borrowed my parents' Ford van with their 22-foot camper trailer hooked up behind it. I had $1,000 of my dad's cash in my pocket. I picked up Uwe's assistant, a very big guy named Arno from the airport. Arno spoke no English, but I spoke German. I was a skinny 21-year-old man with long hair and huge glasses, about to embark on an exciting business adventure. I called a commercial real estate broker in Dallas to line up warehouses to look at. Arno and I drove off to Dallas.

One night in February 1975, while driving on I-20 West, as we reached the crest of a hill, we saw Dallas, a shiny bright modern city shimmering in the night. We were excited. Once we arrived in Dallas, we set up the camper trailer at a KOA campground at Highway 360 in the middle of nowhere, with only a helicopter plant across the street.

I drove 20 miles to meet with Doug, the commercial real estate broker. We drove around to check out several warehouses. After leaving the second one, we were driving down Irving Boulevard talking about the third one, when I turned my head to the right and looked out the window.

"Wait, Doug, turn around now!"

He asked, "What for?"

"That's the place! Right there!"

"It's not even on the list."

"I don't care if it's not on the list. That's the warehouse I want."

Then I told him about my vision.

After securing my dream location, I knew I had two 40-foot shipping containers arriving at the warehouse within 10 days, with a $2,000 invoice owed on each. I just spent almost all of my dad's $1,000 on security deposits for the warehouse. I needed those containers full of antiques. I couldn't sell from an empty space. I had no choice.

I did not want to write checks without having money in the bank, but I had to. I needed those containers full of antiques immediately. I scrambled to sell enough to cover the checks. Fortunately, I sold just enough to cover the checks. I was starving for the first few months with very little business, and I couldn't pay any rent or any of the other bills.

Then I remembered my brief chance meeting with the California importer back in West Berlin. I took my last $250, called the *Dallas Morning News* display advertising department, and asked them to send their photographer as fast as possible. When the photographer showed up, I had him take a series of photos of every type of piece of furniture: wall clocks, grandfather clocks, buffets, nightstands, everything. I gave him ad copy for each piece, coded it, gave him the headlines and my logo along with the last of my money, and placed the display ad.

I was going to use Kmart advertising strategy to sell imported German antiques.

I was 21 years old and under so much stress that when I went to the barber to get a haircut, a big chunk of hair fell out and never grew back. I checked myself into the emergency room because I felt so bad. When the doctor checked my pulse and blood pressure, he said, "Son, I don't know what you're doing, but if you don't stop immediately, you will not see your 22nd birthday."

That was a serious reality check! I decided to breathe deeply, say my prayers, and try to stay calm.

I adopted that philosophy for the rest of my life.

Every few days, I stamped hundreds of postage-paid 3-by-5 cards, and hand wrote the addresses of more than 300 Dallas and Ft. Worth antique dealers. I kept stamping and handwriting another 300 cards every few days and mailed them. Then another batch, and another and another. I was getting writer's cramp. A few more customers showed up and purchased some furniture, then clocks.

After three months of being cooped up 20 miles away from the warehouse in the camper trailer, we needed to be closer to work. I found a cheap one-bedroom unfurnished apartment only a mile away from the warehouse. For several months we slept on a couple of mattresses on the floor, and I kept saying my prayers.

The huge turning point came when an anesthesiologist and his wife walked through the door and bought a life-sized bronze statue of the Virgin Mary for $5,000. Over the next few months, that one couple purchased more than $50,000 of antiques from me.

I consistently ran Sunday display ads weekly with outrageous loss-leader *Sunday Only* specials. For example, I would say, *This Sunday Only! Buy a $400 antique carved armoire for $1.00!* I hung a very large sales tag on that one piece with a perforated lower tag for the lucky buyer to tear off. When I showed up early each Sunday morning, 50 cars were parked in front of the warehouse, and a line of people with a $1.00 bill in their hand stood in front, waiting for me to open the doors.

Everywhere you go, the road to success is under construction.

Then I put a long box full of red *SOLD* tags at the front door and ran *New Shipment Unloading Sale* specials. It created a crazy buying frenzy. As we would unload each piece of furniture and carry it down a long hallway between throngs of salivating buyers, three or four sold tags would get slapped onto each piece. I had to sort out who put their tag on first.

What a problem to have.

Finally, several fist fights broke out and I had to stop that type of sale promotion. That year, I averaged $30,000 to $40,000 per month in sales and that was a lot of money back then.

About this time, our family friend Fred, to whom I'd described my vision two years earlier in Alabama, showed up for a brief visit. When he drove up and got out of the car, his eyes were big and his mouth was wide open. He could not believe what he was looking at—a replica of what I described for him back at the Holiday Inn in Gadsden, Alabama.

Persistence, grit, determination, sacrifice, and hard work, and lots of prayers finally brought me success. After struggling for almost a year, I went from famine to feast. I learned a great deal from those experiences and my journey. It changed my life and my mind set. If you have a dream, faith in God, believe in yourself, and work your butt off executing your plan, you can achieve success in anything you choose to pursue. Action cures fear. Discard doubt and fear and just press on.

You must trust your gut! You must trust people. You must trust God. You must dig your heels in and push and persist no matter what and not quit! Just keep pushing, work hard and get up each morning and then do it again, and again, and again…until you succeed.

Never quit.

Period.

Remember, just when you think you are at your wit's end, on your last straw, on your last penny, at your last bit of sanity, that is when you need to push a little bit more to achieve success!

Biography

Bernard Beausoleil

Bernard "Bernie" Beausoleil is an international entrepreneur and a speaker, author, licensed public insurance adjuster, networker, Eagle Scout, Air Force and Berlin Brat, world traveler, adventurer, and caregiver. He and Debbie, his ex-wife, are proud parents of Nathan and Lauren, who are both in the television and movie industry.

Bernard was born in Scotland to career U.S. Air Force Sergeant Normand "Frenchy" and British mother Joan Beausoleil. He has six younger siblings, Briand, Gerald, Mark, Luke, Sue, and Pauline.

He has launched and built several businesses, including a European antique import business, Houston's first internet cafe with live entertainment, oil and gas industry development, and a distributor network, and has trained and mentored associates in Mexico, Spain, Italy, Guatemala, United Kingdom, and India.

Bernard is a contributing author to Cold War Memories: A Retrospective on Living in Berlin, by Yoshika Loftin Lowe and Trisha A. Lindsey.

Contact Information

Email: BernieBeauAdventure@gmail.com
Website: www.bernardbeausoleil.com
Facebook: bernard beausoleil
Instagram: @berniebeauadventure

CHAPTER FOURTEEN

'Hurt' Versus 'Injured'

Charles L. Brembry, II

More than half of my life was spent in what soldiers call the Profession of Arms, supporting and defending the Constitution of the United States. I was a healthy, able-bodied 19-year-old man when I joined the U.S. Air Force. Twenty years, seven months, and six days later, I retired, a bit worse for wear and brimming with *life experience*—which is a euphemism for all the aches and pains you hear old veterans mention as their joints seize up.

On the surface, I looked like a reasonably healthy, able-bodied 40-year-old man when I left the Air Force.

Iconic movies such as *The Program* and *G.I. Jane* have broken down the difference between what is *hurt* versus what it is to be *injured*. If you are hurt, you may or may not need any kind of minor medical treatment, but an injury requires some type of serious treatment.

Athletes are generally the visible examples in these scenarios. When athletes are hurt, they can shake it off or suck it up and play. When they are injured, all bets are off. They might have to rest for the injury to heal, go through surgery then rehabilitation, or even worse, face forced retirement. You can bounce back from being hurt, but you must recover from an injury. The change in your body resulting from an injury is permanent. You may eventually heal, but you will never be the person you were before the injury.

You just have to make up your mind and seek the help you need.

Athletes suffer in the spotlight, but servicemen and women suffer in the shadows. I'll explain what *hurt versus injured* looks like to this serviceman.

The night of May 6, 2009, I was in a Philadelphia hotel room, getting ready for the next day's training. Around 8 p.m., when my stomach started to hurt, I just chalked it up to eating new food in a new city. Though I was still in pain around midnight, I was finally able to doze off. Around 4 a.m., I awoke with the worst stomach cramps I'd ever experienced. Slowly and painfully, I dressed, drank some Gatorade because I figured I must be dehydrated, and left for class.

I was in so much pain it took me 25 minutes to walk a quarter mile from the military depot gates to the building where classes were held. I bypassed the classroom and went directly to the infirmary, where the nurse on duty explained that pain on the right side *might* be my appendix. She reassured me I'd know for sure if and when I passed out from the pain.

When I finally made it to class, the other students told me I looked bad—so bad, the instructor had one of my fellow students take me to the hospital—against my wishes. This was in 2009, at the peak of the avian influenza pandemic that had begun in Asia. I was stationed in Okinawa and was in Philadelphia just for this week-long class. The ER personnel put me through extra screening to rule out the "bird flu" because I'd just arrived from Asia.

They determined that my appendix had already perforated and they needed to remove it immediately. I was officially *injured*. My surgery was on May 7, and my class visited me in the hospital after graduation on May 8.

The next day was the Saturday, the day before Mother's Day, and I checked myself out against doctor's orders so I could be with my mother that Sunday. At that point, because my injury was repaired, I was only *hurt*, and free to do what I needed to do. Post-surgery, my only concern was getting medically cleared to support the humanitarian Operation Pacific Angel in Timor Leste (East Timor) in June and a contingency deployment for Operation Enduring Freedom to Afghanistan in August.

With five deployments to combat zones under my belt, including two to Iraq, I hoped for something new.

Afghanistan didn't happen, but I was able to deploy to Guantanamo Bay, Cuba. I sucked it up and performed because I was a 32-year-old man who was merely hurt.

Six years later, on the weekend of May 16, I started having pains in my left arm and chest, and additional pain whenever I inhaled. I knew it wasn't a heart attack; it just hurt, but the pain seemed to be getting worse. I called the clinic to see if I could get in for an appointment, but they couldn't see me that week so I just let it go. A couple of days later, the pain got worse, and when I called the clinic again, the triage nurse told me to get to the emergency room immediately.

After they ran a battery of tests, the doctor came in to say they were admitting me because I had several pulmonary embolisms. I let the doctor know that at the ripe age of 38, I wanted a DNR/AND order (do not resuscitate/allow natural death). During my four days in the hospital, I was asked at least twelve times, "Did you request this order and do you know what it means?"

Yes. I did.

I honestly didn't care if I died in that hospital bed or if I was released to die in my bed at home. You may not realize that depression hits in so many ways and looks different in each person. From the outside looking in, most people would think I had a pretty good life. Two months before, I had received a major promotion. Four months before that, I had earned my master's degree. I owned two homes, my car was paid off, and my children were all healthy.

Yet, when I was in the dark place that I was in at that moment, my family, privileges, and awards weren't even on my radar. Not only was I physically injured by the pulmonary embolisms, I was mentally injured with Post-Traumatic Stress Disorder (PTSD) from my previous eight deployments. I didn't yet know about the PTSD because it wouldn't be diagnosed for several months.

Meanwhile, I was cycling through quite a few prescriptions for anti-depression and anti-anxiety medications, trying to find the right fit. In the past few years, I had experienced injuries with my shoulders and lower extremities, all requiring physical therapy and surgery. My injuries, combined with my insomnia and depression, and I felt like my body was shutting down on me. Being taken down with pulmonary embolisms was the last straw.

This time, I was in no position to put up a fight mentally like I had the last time I'd been hospitalized. For some reason, a man at 38 doesn't rebound as fast as he did at 32. Go figure. My last two deployments to Afghanistan had added more than 14 months of stress on top of my previous six deployments.

It inevitably took its toll on my body and my mind. I was injured.

The next eight months were a blur of peaks and valleys—more medications, more rehabilitation, more diagnoses, and more decisions. I have always been a pretty consistent drinker so much so that during medical appointments I was regularly asked, was I interested in inpatient alcohol rehabilitation. Alcohol, of course, is a depressant. And now I was throwing anti-depressant prescription drugs into the mix and I faced the multiplier effect, a phenomenon where one item that is input causes larger changes on other factors in the equation. It's basically synergy in the worst form.

I admit that during that period in my life I didn't make the soundest decisions concerning my personal safety but I was trying to numb my pain. When I finally decided to seek help, I went through a lengthy Question and Answer session about things that I had been saying and notations in my medical records for the last 13 years. I began meeting with a Licensed Specialist Clinical Social Worker who showed me coping techniques and plans to deal with my PTSD and depression. I also began to cut back on my alcohol consumption as well. There is no cure for PTSD, but some people learn to manage it and/or avoid stressors. Prescription medications do help some, but not all, of those afflicted.

Many people believe they know me, but they only know certain parts of me—the parts I let them know. I have been told too often that I distance myself and compartmentalize my life. After hearing this refrain time after time, I finally was forced to realize, "I guess it *is* me, because everyone can't be wrong."

Those folks *were* right. I am a very secretive person. For instance, when I decided I was going to be my own boss after I retired from the military, that I would explore the world of full-time entrepreneurship, I only told a handful of the people to whom I felt closest. I held the information back not because I was ashamed of my choice, but so our conversations wouldn't be awkward.

I don't like crowds and unfamiliar people. I generally prefer to avoid "new people" and also familiar people in groups. After doing some reading, I believe the term *anti-*

social extrovert—someone who is energized by other people but faces great anxiety when in social situations—describes me quite well. I like people but they vex me quite often. I have been known to enter and exit an event simultaneously *hello*-ing while *goodbye*-ing! It's a gift or a curse, but it's me.

For all of my adult life, I worked in a beehive without much free thought, just orders and compliance. I knew I wanted to become an entrepreneur after my military career ended even before I knew my retirement date.

I made the decision to dramatically change my career path after attending an Orlando entrepreneurship conference in January 2016. If you attended the conference, you will remember how self-affirming the event was. I knew at that moment that entrepreneurship was the life for me, and I didn't care what anyone said about it. Once I retired, I wouldn't be taking orders or asking for permission from anyone. At that life-changing international event, I knew I had found my calling, my purpose, and my next career.

At that point, I still planned to make Chief Master Sergeant and retire after 24 years of dedicated service. After a couple of months, my plan lost traction when I was removed from my position as squadron superintendent via a phone call while I was on vacation. Who gets fired on their vacation?

That wasn't as terrifying as it probably seems; instead, it was my defining pivotal moment. The abrupt change would have broken many people to the point of no return. When it comes to retiring from the military, many folks find it hard to walk away. Once they leave, many feel a lack of purpose. Rather than being mad, upset, and enraged,

I was briefly hurt—literally, for five minutes—and then I was ecstatic. I had already scheduled a trip the next week to one of the top resorts in Mexico and I was looking forward to it, without thinking a moment about work.

There were other happy consequences, as well. I was better able to focus on making decisions for my future, and I was introduced to some great new supportive coworkers.

That demotion was the nudge from God I needed to transition on to something much better for my family and me. For the next 30 days, I debated whether I should retire, and in May 2016, I finally made the decision to push the button. The soonest I could retire was March 1, 2017 and I knew that it would be a long wait full of annoying questions about my future.

The next 10 months was an endless loop of *Are you sure you're ready to retire? Can you afford to retire? Are you gonna be a GS? Where are you gonna work?* After being in the military for more than 20 years, I realized many people only know work, work, work. Leave a job, get a job, retire from a job, get another job, retire again, then die within five years.

I knew I hadn't lived this long to become another statistic or to live a life of anything other than what I dreamed it should be. While many people are outwardly cocky or confident, most really don't believe in themselves. Though I had spent my adult life in the military, I never defined myself by the uniform or the titles. I wasn't losing my self-image, and it wasn't going to hurt when I gave it up. When folks asked me about my retirement plans, I kept it simple: "Some traveling. Whatever I want to do."

Retirement from the military was one of the best decisions of my life, and I have not regretted it. I only question why I didn't decide to do it sooner. My choice to become an entrepreneur puts me in a position to help even more people than I could when I was in the military.

My retirement, while glorious, has come with its own set of challenges. Some days tend to be better than others. At the flip of a switch, my underlying PTSD can cause my happy demeanor to turn into hypervigilance, and I must sometimes leave a situation because I become overwhelmed by the crowds. It doesn't happen often and I know how to deal with it, but I tend to miss some important things. I'm not able to take my children to fireworks events; I have trouble with explosions. I missed my mentor's keynote speech in Charlotte in 2017 because my PTSD kicked in and I felt overwhelmed and stressed.

I've put a lot of thought into how I developed PTSD. It appears I went through phases. When you arrive on deployment, it's natural to be anxious or nervous while getting to know your surroundings. Then you move to being confident while still aware you are in a dangerous place. Finally, you get somewhat apathetic to the violence, while still trying to keep those around you safe. During one of my shortest deployments, I remember reports of possible mustard gas attacks, plus 114 actual mortar attacks; we kept track of them in the office with hash marks.

In Iraq, they attacked anytime, day or night. In the early morning, we were repeatedly mortared, and attacks mean loud sirens, followed by donning chemical, biological, radiological, nuclear, and explosive gear plus flak jacket.

You must do this within seconds while helping your wingman or battle buddy get dressed, all without knowing the threat. Next, you must go outside and sweep the area for unexploded ordinance, casualties, or suspicious items, and report the status.

Can you imagine doing that multiple times every day while working 12-hour shifts six days a week for up to 210 days straight?

You carry a handgun or a rifle 24/7 as well. It was normal to see people bench pressing with a gun strapped on their hip, or to see a lone hand holding a rifle muzzle while the rest of their body is hidden behind a shower curtain. When you go home, you reacclimate to not carrying a weapon constantly, and to not ducking under furniture when you hear a siren.

On my last deployment in Kabul, I completed more than 100 convoys. Can you imagine riding in a bulletproof SUV, wearing full battle rattle—helmet, flak jacket, gloves, knee pads, elbow pads, radio, rifle, handgun, and sometimes more—depending on the mission? Now picture yourself in chaotic traffic, with people panhandling everywhere, traffic signals and signs treated as suggestions, all the while keeping alert and viewing everything around you as a possible threat.

There's also a difference between seeing a peacefully deceased person in a casket versus seeing a fellow serviceman's charred body in a body bag. The level of loss you feel when you see the flag flying at half-staff for a person who ate with you the day before can't be put into words.

The impressions on your brain don't vanish overnight. I've had mine for more than a decade.

When I share my story, I don't ask anyone who's never been injured to relate to my injuries, but I do ask those who do relate to realize there's a positive way out of the situation. Whether you are a retiree, veteran, on active duty, or civilian, you can shake off being hurt, and you can definitely recover from physical and mental injuries, no matter what the cause. You just have to make up your mind and seek the help you need.

There are many helping hands and agencies just waiting for your call. . . *so pick up the phone.*

Biography

Born and raised in Dallas, Charles L. Brembry, II always had a gift for public speaking and helping others. After a short stint at Texas A&M University, he enlisted in the U.S. Air Force. Charles served on deployments to Guantanamo Bay and multiple tours to Iraq and Afghanistan, and he earned many awards including the Bronze Star. He served an active duty commitment lasting for more

Charles L. Brembry, II

than 20 years, retiring honorably from the U.S. Air Force in 2017.

Throughout his career, Charles dedicated himself to higher education, earning three Associate Degrees, a B.S. in Management Studies, and a M.S. in Acquisition and Contract Management.

His new career as an entrepreneur has Charles expanding into multiple fronts, and he hopes to use the skills he acquired through Johnny Wimbrey's mentorship to help change the lives of future generations. He is also an avid traveler and travel blogger.

Charles has returned to Dallas and shares joint custody of his four children. He enjoys mentoring and speaking to youth as well as to other military veterans suffering from PTSD-related conditions.

Contact information

Website: www.clbrembry.com
Facebook: www.facebook.com/cl.brembry2
Instagram: @mr7dywknd
Twitter: @CLBrembry

CHAPTER FIFTEEN

Make a Difference

Ashley L. Burton

My goal is to inspire others! I want my family, my friends, and my associates to know that I am not just the sum of my past or some woman with issues. Yes, I have tattoos. Yes, I have a tough attitude, but it did not come from me trying to be someone else. It came from being a survivor.

Today, my children come first, and I will do everything in my power to give them the life I never had. I want them to be able to be children for as long as possible and not grow up too quickly; to learn responsibility, yet not have to face adult choices. I know my kids love me and that's what keeps me going.

I want to share my background and let people know that mine is a story of strength, faith, and everything else that made me into the woman I am today. I have so many goals to accomplish and I'm just getting started.

Sometimes, I laugh to myself and say, *I really did it.* While I'm driving, I also smile for no reason and say, *God is good* and *thank you!*

I feel no shame in praising the Lord. I have my own beliefs and know how I feel about God. I don't go to church and I don't feel like I need to go to church to have faith and believe in Him. My parents took me to church when I was growing up, and I had my first communion at Saint Leo's Church in Leominster, Massachusetts.

No more! Today I will break the cycle. I will not be a victim of my past and will instead make my own new path.

As an adult, I've attended church on and off on my own for years. When I attended regularly, I was running from the hurt and pain of what I was going through, and I was asking for help. Instead, faith should be in all aspects of our lives, not just when we are in church, when we're having a few hard days, or when our life is going downhill. I'm not against being part of organized religion, because church is an amazing feeling when we go, and feeling that comfort after praising Him is great. I'm just saying what I noticed in my attendance and my family's.

There's been a lot of running away by my family members and by me. We tend to run away from everything.

My heart is very loving, but it's been shattered like a mirror. It's in millions of pieces. I wonder how I still love, care, and give constructive criticism toward others without sadness overwhelming me. I question why I keep smiling and keep being happy. You know that saying, *a person who hides behind a beautiful smile can be dying inside?* Well, that was me.

I am not asking for your pity, because accepting pity is not my forte.

My history has a lot of tragedy and pain, and that was all I knew in life. Concealing my pain became part of my every action when I was a child. I saw terrible things, like going with my mother to pick up her next fix, and my dad being violent and drunk, beating my mother. The traumas I have witnessed, such my mother overdosing, became part of my fabric, my cycle of living, and I believed they were a part of every child's life.

I am here today and God has made sure I wasn't going anywhere just yet. I am apparently not done with my journey. I am here for reasons yet to be revealed.

When my mom died, I realized life is way too short. Her death triggered my decision to stop mistreating myself—with my relationships, my job, and my friendships. I was used to making everyone around me happy or satisfied. That's all I had been to everyone for my entire life—the person who made everyone happy. I was tired of proving to friends and loved ones that I was loyal and a wonderful person.

All I ever wanted was to be liked and loved. I always wondered why people didn't like me or even hated me, why

I was being bullied, or why someone fought with me because they didn't like me.

Why?

Why? is the question I always asked myself.

I asked God why those things happened to me. When I was very young, I also asked Him why I was still alive and on earth, because there were times when I didn't want to be alive anymore.

I had figured things out on my own for most of my life.

When I was a young child, I was in and out of foster homes, constantly surrounded by domestic violence, drugs, and dangerous or bad situations. When I was 10 years old, I was living on Pleasant Street in Leominster, where I lived off and on while growing up. My aunt and my mother were always together even when getting high in the bathroom.

One day, I went into the bathroom when they were done. When I sat down on the toilet, I noticed a shoelace and a syringe in the wastebasket to the right of me. I reached into the basket, grabbed the shoestring, and picked up the needle. I'd witnessed my mother and family shoot up many times, so I knew what to do, and I decided to follow suit, right then and there. Once I tied the shoestring around my left bicep, I touched the needle to the inside of my elbow where my vein was exposed. I was ready to follow their example.

Suddenly I stopped. In a panic, I threw the syringe back into the wastebasket, untied the shoelace, and rushed out of the bathroom. I pretended nothing had happened—

pretended I hadn't almost turned my life into a living hell, the same heroin hell that most of my family shared.

I have worked in the medical field for the last 13 years, and during that time, I've made a point of speaking to people about my experiences in life. It's rewarding to be able to help others by sharing my stories.

My passion is to inspire people who have dealt with personal addiction, family addiction, and domestic violence, and be a voice for them. I know the fear people face when they are dealing with those issues. Survivors are often afraid to use their voices. I want to support men and women who have had traumatic experiences in their lives and to help guide them so they can understand they don't have to carry that fear with them forever. I want to help them learn from the past and say, *No more! Today I will break the cycle. I will not be a victim of my past and will instead make my own new path!*

I founded Mentor, a non-profit agency that supports men, women and children who are survivors of domestic violence and serves as a voice for others when they don't have one. Both men and women are victims of domestic violence, and I want to help survivors of both genders. I want to be a voice in the courts and shelters for battered men and women because *I too* have been denied a restraining order and was too afraid to continue with court action because of fear of retaliation by past partners. I was denied a restraining order against my former partner, who was being released after serving a prison term for a gun charge. I was told that if I wanted to be safe, I would have to leave the home where I'd lived with my children for more than five years and move into a shelter. Instead, I refused to leave the home and continued to fight for my rights.

The situation was unfair to my children and me; a move meant we would be starting over. It was just wrong, and that's why I say *NO MORE* will I be a victim; I will stand strong and fight for my own rights as a single mother of two kids. I am tired of running, and I won't do it anymore. I will not hide in the shadows as I have always done. I will no longer be made to feel that I am beneath these men.

And in turn, I will help others who are going through the same trauma. I believe domestic violence should be treated far more seriously by law enforcement, the courts, and by society. Domestic violence is often fatal; it takes just one second for an abusive partner or spouse to pull a trigger or harm you physically, long before assistance has a chance to arrive.

I was an abused woman for a long time. Now it's time to share my story, to help others in that situation know they can push through and survive, too. I want survivors to know how amazing it is on the other side. Their smiles will be brighter, their hearts will beat differently, and they will have their glow on! Believe me, that brilliance is inside of every man or woman and they sometimes just need help to reach in and find it.

Despite everything, I am here today and it's a phenomenal feeling that I never thought I would experience. I never expected to be where I am today.

I finally realized how tenacious and determined I could be, how I could really P.U.S.H., when I decided to go to rehab in Worcester, Massachusetts. I'd hit bottom, losing my apartment and my son in one night because I had been selling drugs. I was homeless, and getting my son back seemed almost impossible since the caseworkers knew my entire family history and were waiting for me to fail. It didn't matter. At that moment I had one purpose in life: get my son back and get him out of foster care, the "system."

I'd discovered that going through rehab was the only way I could get my child back. Though I'd sold drugs, I never used them. I did smoke marijuana, but since I wasn't an addict, the facility wouldn't accept me at first. Finally, I lied and said I was an alcoholic in order to be admitted.

At rehab, I did everything they wanted me to do. I was a model client in every way, and I spent a great deal of time listening to the people who were suffering from addiction. Hearing their stories was like watching the lives of my family members unfold around me. I broke down when I felt the pain in one man as he shared his story, and it helped me began to appreciate life more fully.

What I learned in rehab made me more determined than ever to regain custody of my one-year-old son. I pushed myself hard, full of resolve to get him back, out of the system, and to give him a safe home with me. When I "graduated" from rehab, I refused to leave. I told the administrators, "I'm not leaving until I am approved for residential treatment; I know I need it to get my son back." I knew sitting on a friend's couch, homeless and waiting for a residential program, was not going to further my cause with Social Services. I was determined to get back on track as quickly as possible.

There was a waiting list for residential programs, though, so I couldn't go directly from rehab to the program. I was sent to a holding facility for people waiting to get into halfway houses and programs in a nearby town, which is where I stayed until a spot opened in a residential program.

For the next 30 days, I waited in the holding facility, basically on my own with very little support, doing my best to jump through all the right hoops to get my son back. I applied for welfare because everyone had to help supply our own food while we lived there, and a staff member drove me to the Social Services office.

Waiting to be picked up outside the office, I noticed a huge brick building across the street, about six stories high and with lots of windows. When I craned my head back and looked all the way up at the last row of windows, I saw the word BELIEVE spelled backward in the window. All the other windows were blank.

In a flash, I knew my life was going to be different. I didn't know how or what, but I realized that moment was my spiritual awakening. For the first time in my life, I understood serenity.

In that moment, I knew the path my children's lives would take didn't need to follow the path I'd taken so far. I knew I must keep fighting and never give up, no matter how difficult things became in my life.

Today, I still hear from some friends and family members who believed I would grow up to be a life-long drug dealer, addicted to drugs, and in and out of jail. I came close, but instead I turned my life around. Today I realize that I *can* make a difference. I show people that they, too, can make a difference—if they want to do so.

As a positive role model, taking action to improve my life and the lives of my children, I know I've helped many people. Many of them ask me, "How do you do it?"

My answer is always the same. "I want a better life for my family, so I just go for what I want in life. I get it, and you can, too."

I have been able to overcome the difficult challenges in my life. I've found myself, finally learned to love myself, and have accepted that I'm valuable to other people as well. As I walk in faith every day, I see that many doors have opened for me.

It keeps getting better. Now it's my time to help others.

I'm here and ready to share my life with the world.

Everything is possible.

Biography

Ashley L. Burton

Ashley L. Burton is the founder of Mentor, a non-profit organization that supports and advocates for victims of domestic violence and families with a history of drug addiction or broken homes. She has worked with The Mom's Project in Boston, Massachusetts, which works with single mothers who are trying to improve their lives.

By sharing her life experiences, Ashley hopes to help women who have experienced similar events but cannot see a way out of it. She believes that it's never too late to make a change in your life or to assist someone you care about.

She graduated from Everest College with a degree in medical administration, and has worked in the medical field for 13 years.

Ashley and her two amazing children, Natavies and Jayaniese, live in Hingham, Massachusetts.

Contact Information

Email: ashleyburton713@yahoo.com
Facebook: Ashley Burton
Instagram: @Ashleylynn_32
Blog: Ashleysjourney.com

Breaking the Generational Curse

CaDaryl A. Atkins

My parents don't get much credit for raising me, though I love them and I'm glad they both are part of my adult life. I was raised mostly by a grandmother and great-grandmother who cared enough to build my moral underpinnings and make me who I am today. They helped me break the generational curse that damaged so many in our family.

My three younger brothers and I had different fathers who never were present in our lives. The four of us were raised in a household of 13, including aunts, uncles, grandparents, and cousins. My grandmother, whom I called Big Mama, and my great-grandmother, Rodessa, were strong ladies with deep moral beliefs, and they kept the peace in the family.

Almost every family in our small town of Mansfield, Louisiana, lived in poverty. A typical day had some family in my neighborhood borrowing sugar or even a package of meat from someone else lucky enough to have extra. To make matters worse, I grew up in the 1980s when the crack epidemic was in full effect. A lot of people were chasing highs and doing absolutely whatever they needed, to experience that feeling over and over, and the people distributing crack were glad that the thirst for the drug existed.

When you have a desire to do something and your positive actions are greater than your excuses, *anything* is possible.

Of the thirteen people in my home, three were on drugs as well as my father, who cut my hair and was my barber before I ever knew he was my father. Don't forget the alcoholics—almost half of the people in my neighborhood were alcoholics.

There I was, a little boy with a special conscience. I had a desire to want to fit in and be like everyone else, but my reality made me stand out. My great-grandma and aunts did what they could to keep us rooted in church, but the terrible things I saw challenged my faith greatly. I believe there are certain things I shouldn't have witnessed as a child, like being told by your mother to lay down on the back seat of a car while she and her friends smoked crack in the front seat. Like to be numb to the hurt you felt from seeing that familiar jittery, bloodshot look of highness and paranoia in a loved one's eyes, and you know that's not who they are. Like finding broken antennas and pipes wrapped with foil and stuffed with pot scrubbing material. Like sneaking to check out your Christmas present, seeing that your aunts bought you and your brothers the latest Nintendo, hoping for it Christmas morning, but anticipating you'll find out your mom stole and sold your game. Like food and anything that wasn't nailed down being stolen just to buy that next rock of crack. Like watching family members borrowing money, knowing they had no intention of paying it back.

I had always had this dream of being a superhero, saving my family by making a lot of money, moving them away, and helping everybody get on their feet.

When our food was stolen, we went to the candy lady and got something on credit for our meal. Sometimes I didn't see my mother for weeks. That was probably good in the long run, though, because in her absence my great-grandmother was able to introduce great morals into my life. She did her best to teach me how to be a gentleman and a good man in spite of the hell going on around us.

I tended to be shy, reserved, and standoffish when it came to school, but inside that shy kid was a young man with a great sense of humor who could make anybody smile even when it was hard to do so myself. At school, I compared my life to those of other kids my age. Even in our poor town, most had nice clothes and shoes I only had heard about and never dreamed I'd own. People joked a lot at my school, and the last thing I wanted to do was draw attention to the cheap clothes that I wore. It didn't matter how quiet I was, I still got picked on a lot.

The values my grandparents taught me didn't help my esteem at all in school, not until I was more mature. My great-grandma always told me to look out for my brothers, but I didn't know how, and I never had a father to show me how to look out for myself and others. My uncles stepped in and did their best to teach me those skills despite their own bad habits. So there I was, growing up, trying to be somewhat grateful and comfortable in this painful situation, and at the same time, blend in and act normal like other kids.

I had always had this dream of being a superhero, saving my family by making a lot of money, moving them away, and helping everybody get on their feet—a dream of truly living life for what it should be. Little did I know there was a storm brewing with my name on it.

The summer I was ten, a cloud came over my life when my three brothers and I were picked up by Child Protective Services (CPS). When they came to our house to check on us, as they had been doing for some time now, they checked the refrigerator. It was empty but for a Cornish hen and a pack of dry salted meat. We hadn't eaten yet and we were on our way to a summer feeding program to eat a big dinner. CPS picked us up that evening in front of the whole neighborhood as we kicked and screamed, "I don't wanna go!" But no matter how loudly we screamed, our cries were ignored. The living situation at our house was considered unsafe for us children.

We were taken to a holding facility where we sat, trying to figure out if this was just a nightmare, and wondering what the next moment would bring. Both questions remained unanswered and would puzzle us for the next few hours. Even at ten years old, I was a person who always tried to look at the positive side of things. I'm thinking, "Okay, what do I know about foster homes?" I remembered only good thoughts, but I didn't realize my perception was not my reality. They split my brothers and me up; I was sent to Benton, an even smaller town about an hour away from Mansfield. They sent my baby brother, who was only about five or six years old, to Shreveport, about 30 minutes away. They sent my twin brothers to a home on the outskirts of our town, about ten minutes away from our home. The twins, who were about nine, were able to continue at the same school.

I was in a situation where I no longer could be a big brother. I had to survive in this new place that I knew nothing about. I went in with a positive attitude, thinking everything would be cool. CPS had told us to hang on for just three months and we would be home. At first things seemed fine, but the three older boys already in the foster home became jealous of the attention I was getting as a newbie and warned me, "This isn't really how it is; don't let our foster mother trick you."

Soon I found out what they meant. It was like coming out of a nightmare that you became accustomed to and going into another one you know absolutely nothing about. I was going through some of the same problems I had going on back at home, but with a different spin.

The foster house was on a dead end street and there were no kids around us except for my foster brothers. I was surrounded by woods and a few older foster relatives who lived in the cul-de-sac. There was no contact with the outside world. As the woman who was my foster mother gradually introduced me to my new reality, I had to quickly adjust and get into survival mode. There were times I had to dig deep to find and listen to my grandparents' voices.

I was now in a place where I was constantly told I could never accomplish this or never be that. I was always reminded that my own mother didn't want me. I began to believe it was true because months were long gone and here I was, still trapped in this unreal life I couldn't escape.

My grandma had told me, "If you have a problem with something or someone, then talk it out, get an understanding." So I reached out to my social worker. When she turned around and told my foster mother about my claims, of course she denied them. Everything backfired and I started getting treated harshly, as though I'd broken a code. I thought often about running away, and at times, suicidal thoughts even crossed my mind. I did my best to continue to remain humble and patient because that's really all I had left.

Big Mama and my Aunt Schanay bought a manufactured home to create a safe environment for us four boys away from the chaos of the rest of the family, and we were released from foster care the day before my eleventh birthday on June 22, 1998. I now had to start growing up fast and make a lot of good decisions, so I set out on a journey to free myself, release my gifts to the world, and figure out how life worked. My journey became an ongoing, lifelong experience that is responsible for who I really am today.

My mother was in rehab at the time, and I knew my grandparents were getting old, and at some point, they wouldn't be there physically to push me and help me when I needed encouragement. In the time we would have together, I had to learn all that I could. My grandmother and great-grandma died back-to-back a few years after I got out of foster care, but they never left me; in fact, it seems as though they came alive inside me. They often talked to me, encouraging me and letting me know that everything would be okay.

My family started attending Higher Ground Ministries, an awesome nondenominational church where I met Pastor Ronnie Morris, Sr. He was a great mentor in my life during that key time after foster care. I had a lot of insecurities and self-esteem problems, and he instilled confidence in me that I'd lacked. He made me aware of qualities I didn't know I had, and he made me view myself in a totally different way. I began to feel as though I had a purpose and it was greater than me.

Pastor Ronnie taught me that anything I believe in is possible. He also prophesied that I would take the stage in front of crowds and that many, both young and old, would look up to me. He taught me how to draw people with the cords of love. My destiny awaited me and it was up to me to go get it.

In church, I became very active. I rapped, sang in the choir, taught classes, and went to juvenile centers to speak to troubled youth and offer them the plan of salvation. It felt good to be able to encourage other young people and give them hope for a better tomorrow.

During my teenage years. I found that playing football was always a way for me to get rid of stress. I had built up so much stress to that point, I became good at football—so good that when I graduated in 2005, I had several scholarships. Though I wasn't enthusiastic about college, I chose Southern Arkansas University.

I admit the psychology courses interested me because I wanted to learn more about people, the way the brain, energy, vibrations, and manifestations work, and why people act the way they act. I learned to manifest whatever it is I wanted by sending positive energy toward it, acting as though it's already mine and letting the universe do the rest for me. I often found myself praying and fasting at a young age and it worked. Later, as my understanding got better, I incorporated meditation and found that it works as well.

I stayed in college one year, until a complication with my scholarship began to create a financial hardship. Next, I studied carpentry at the Shreveport Job Corps Center and picked up other skills that would help me along the way.

Student government was my next step; when I joined, we were required to join Toastmasters International, a group that taught me to speak in public, make eye contact, speak with my hands, control the audience. and how to flow. I picked up social skills from being around so many different people in life and observing the way they behave. I graduated and continued advanced Job Corps training in St. Louis.

When it was time to choose a career, I saw the demand for truck drivers, so I went to driving school in 2008. I've had a chance to see the country and all of its beauty, and I find driving trucks very calming, relaxing, and therapeutic because you have time for deep thoughts while driving.

I can honestly say my struggles helped me to realize

Early in life I learned that knowledge is power.

the true purpose I was placed on this earth to pursue. My purpose is clearly not to only help myself grow, but to help others like me keep pushing ahead.

All my life, I've been told by others that when I got older I would see how I'd have to struggle with bills *because life is hard.* I was told that no matter what I wanted to accomplish, I'd be sidetracked because of financial struggles and kids. I have always been a stickler for proving people wrong, so I begged to differ with the naysayers. My great-grandma always supported my rebellion against these negative thinkers, and she reminded me that I needed to break our family's generational curse so I wouldn't fall victim to it.

My ultimate dream is to have substantial wealth, enough to give me the freedom to spend my time giving motivation and encouragement to crowds of every size, whether it's through comedy or motivational speaking. I want to continue to bless people miraculously on a larger scale and let them know there is still hope for humanity.

When you have a desire to do something and your positive actions are greater than your excuses, *anything* is possible. In pursuit of becoming the great person I am determined to become, I've gone to juvenile centers to mentor youth, share my knowledge and spread encouragement. I've fed homeless people, bought groceries for people, have given away many of my most valuable belongings, and bestowed monetary gifts. I never look for handouts or paybacks in return. My grandmother taught me well. Because of her, I've escaped the family curse and I'm not afraid. I'm living life.

I'm grateful to everyone I mentioned here plus so many more who have played some part in my growth, even though I may have been unaware of it at the time. I'm doing things they said I would never do, going places they said I would never go—*in spite* of what I was told when I was a child.

Because I often had to laugh at my pain to keep from crying, I found making others laugh made me feel good. This led me to comedy, and I've become a stand-up comedian. The majority of my comedy comes from the stories of my life, a laugh-at-my-pain approach to making people laugh until their sides hurt. I moved to Dallas in 2016, looking for bigger venues and audiences.

Early in life I learned that knowledge is power. People like to enjoy learning, and laughter makes it even easier to share my knowledge. I talk seriously or with humor to juvenile and recovery groups, job corps centers, church events—wherever I can help.

Since I've been on my quest for more knowledge and a deeper understanding of how life truly works, I've learned how to live life prosperously through manifestation—which to me means I can have or become anything I can imagine. With a positive attitude, consistency, and dedication, anything I dream I can *become*.

You can *become*, as well.

Biography

CaDaryl A. Atkins

CaDaryl A. Atkins was born on June 23, 1987, in Shreveport, Louisiana, and relocated to the Dallas Metroplex in 2016, where he drives trucks, performs comedy routines, and acts. As a single man in Arlington, Texas, he calls himself a sapiosexual, defined as "a person who finds intelligence to be the most sexually attractive characteristic of another person." He loves to learn, and he enjoys enlightening conversations, especially with older people who provide different perspectives. His outlook on life is always positive.

He's built his stand-up comedy routines around a "laugh-at-my-pain" approach to comedy, and has done improv in Texas and Shreveport, Louisiana. CaDaryl acts, uses social media for funny skits based in truth, and enjoys poetry and writing. His inspirational and motivational speaking to youth and adults is about love, relationships, gaining confidence, and boosting self-esteem.

CaDaryl's extended family includes three brothers and a beloved grandmother, Big Mama.

Contact information

Email: cadarylatkins@yahoo.com
Facebook: CaDaryl Tha Entertainer Atkins
Instagram: @CaDaryl Tha Entertainer Atkins

It's Your Move

Sashin Govender

My childhood in KwaZulu-Natal, Durban, South Africa was spent in a comfortable, relatively prosperous household. My family has been entrepreneurial for generations, and both my parents and grandparents were self-employed. I love saying it's difficult trying to convince an individual to make the shift from self-employed to employee, but it's rather easy to convince them to move from employee to self-employed.

My family is extremely close and loyal, though small: my father, Preggie, my mother, Anita, my older sister Priyanka, two grannies, a handful of aunts, uncles, and cousins.

Early in my life I was tested with adversity, which either breaks you or causes you to break records. My parents separated when I was just two, and I cannot recall my parents sharing the same bed or living under the same roof. The family wasn't completely broken, we just didn't live together. My weekdays were spent with my father's parents and my mom downstairs in a granny flat, weekends with dad, and wherever I was, my sister was in the other household. For my first 18 years, there were no family meals or celebrations with all of us at the same table. My grandparents really were my primary parents, playing a huge role in my foundation. They always went the extra mile for me.

Personal development is food to the soul and mind; personal development saved my life.

My sister and I were always caught in the middle of family arguments and forced to choose sides. I learned to avoid negativity and conflict when I was very young.

Despite these rough spots, my parents have been role models to me; I've taken their good and bad life lessons and learned from their mistakes. Your upbringing is vital—it creates the foundation for your life.

My father always dressed to impress, drove fancy cars, lived in penthouse suites, and dated beautiful woman. My mom found a way to argue with almost every one of his girlfriends, whether behind closed doors or out in public. The public squabbles were embarrassing, turning school and sports award functions or even family gatherings into disasters. Even these embarrassments prepared me to be the person I am today.

Incidentally, I wasn't the smartest kid in the classroom if you define *smart* by what you read, remember, and regurgitate. I was always the last guy to walk into class, the first guy to walk out; I couldn't stop talking. It was as if I only went to school to plan the weekend.

My first true love was sports. At a very young age, I fell in love with cricket, a game somewhat like baseball that is played wherever England had planted its flag at some time. I had the entire neighborhood playing in the street. I'd convince everyone who visited to come outside and throw the ball so I could hit it out of the park. The minute my father or grandfather came from work, rain or shine, they would have to bowl the ball to me until dark.

Whenever possible I attended cricket matches; when I couldn't, I watched them on television. I knew all the professional cricket players and made sure they knew me. I took pictures with them, had dinner with them, got their contact numbers, showed up early before the match to see the team buses arrive, and stayed late to see the team buses depart, then went to their hotel to stalk them.

My dream was to become a professional cricket player, representing South Africa and touring the world. Ironically, my life followed a similar path; I tour the world speaking to sold-out crowds, inspiring and motivating them to take action and chase their dreams and goals.

My second love was chess. On my sixth birthday, my father gave me a board game with checkers on one side of the board and chess on the other. When I opened my gift, it was late in the evening, yet I insisted my father teach me to play chess. The game wasn't easy for me, and it didn't go well that first evening. My father almost threw in the towel and flipped the board over to teach me checkers, but I insisted on learning how to play chess. He spent hours teaching me the value of each piece, how it moves on the board, the purpose of the game, and how to think ahead.

Over the next few days I begged my father to play chess with me for a few hours each day. Soon, I began to adapt and innovate moves on the board, and the moves I learned eventually taught me to adapt and innovate real life circumstances. Chess allowed me to become a visionary and a pioneer. As I became a chess wizard, I learned to adapt and leverage my chess skills in my daily life.

My third love appeared when I was eight years old and I was introduced to the world of personal development. My parents introduced my sister and me to *The Secret*, a movie by Rhonda Byrne, a book called *Mind Power for Children,* and a course called *Making of a Champion.* I learned how to set goals, recite affirmations, create a vision board, and visualize daily. I began to learn how to control my thoughts and feelings and how to manifest things mentally before I materialized them.

CHESS + PERSONAL DEVELOPMENT = UNSTOPPABLE!

My 16-year habit of personal development and 18 years of thinking like a chess player have helped make me mentally strong. I have worked hard to have zero emotional attachment to negativity. Did you know it takes 15 positive thought to counter-attack one negative thought? Why would you even entertain a negative thought, knowing it would take that amount of energy to erase it?

We all have an inner voice which tells us what we should do and how we should do it. I like to call it the complacent version of you, within you. That soft inner voice tries its best to slow you down, yet it can be trained and overpowered by your conscious mind, which is all about feelings and energy.

It's all in the mind. This is the secret that was never taught to us at school. It's never too early to begin personal development.

If you have children, I highly recommend that you start them with personal development *now*. Personal development is food to the soul and mind; personal development saved my life.

YOUR EVOLUTION

Can everyone become successful? I truly believe everyone can, but *will* they become successful?

No.

There's one thing you need to know about me: *I tell the truth.* It might piss you off or it may cause you to trust me. I strongly believe our upbringing and values determine our foundation, and our foundation determines the person we become. Every aspect of our life is trial and error until we find the formula.

I was eight years old when I began the process of trial and error with my life. I spent a long time perfecting my dream life in my mind before I manifested it. It took me 16 years to become an overnight success.

When your preparation coincides with God's timing,

that magic merger creates *momentum*, your inner fire. From then forward, it's game over, but only if you keep that fire burning.

Not enough people realize this key fact: *Your mindset is your largest asset*. Equally, a negative mindset is your biggest disease, one that creeps into your body without you even recognizing it. Most people think cancer, diabetes, and HIV/AIDS are the deadliest diseases, but a negative mindset has a larger impact. Eighty percent of life is psychological; only twenty percent is purely physical.

The mind is our largest and most valuable asset. Thanks to my parents starting me on personal development so young, I've spent most of my life and more than one million South African Rand on developing my foundation.

Did you know the right mindset can cure a disease?

It all begins with a thought. A thought is the seed you plant and desire to sow. The higher your frequency of positivity and energy, the healthier your seeds become. Think about it, diseases generally start from within—you don't notice it until it is eating you from the inside out. When it is too late to cure yourself, you start seeing the symptoms from the outside. You may have cancer in the early stages and still cure it by having an untouchable positive outlook on life.

If you focus on negativity, you'll only attract negative people, energy, and results. If you focus on positivity, you'll attract positive people, energy, and results. It's easier said than done; we are all humans and there's virtually no way to live a positive life 24/7/365. I don't mentor and coach people to be positive all day, I teach people to accept and appreciate negativity, but then counterattack it. I cannot overemphasize, for every negative thought, you'll need fifteen positive thoughts as counterattack. Why would you even consider entertaining negativity?

You might be going through challenges right now in your life, whether it's your health, wealth, spirituality, or even relationships. Let it happen *to* you and not *within* you. Let it hit and bounce off; don't let it in and let it eat you up from inside-out.

How long does it take to think negatively?

A split second!

Your mind is your largest asset. What have you done to protect it from haters, hackers, and people who bring you down? Have you set up a password for your mind?

When you logged into your cellphone today, it required a password.

When you logged into your laptop today, it required a password.

When you logged into your social media accounts today, they required passwords.

When you logged into your email account today, it required a password.

What is the purpose of passwords? To protect your information from hackers and people you don't trust.

You must protect your mind with a password.

SAW = WAS

The word SAW is powerful. Even when I was broke, I saw myself driving dream cars, flying first class around the world, speaking at the AT&T Stadium in front of 25,000-

plus people, living in the former president's house, owning multiple enterprises, having a passive income of seven figures-plus.

When you flip the word SAW = WAS. I *was* there in my mind way before I physically manifested it, I *was* driving those dream cars in my mind before I took delivery of that Ferrari, I *was* flying first class in my mind before I stretched out on that leather seat, I *was* speaking in front of sold-out crowds even before I walked onto that stage at the AT&T Stadium.

It's a surreal feeling when you turn a thought into reality. It might sound impossible, but that's how my life is lived. Millionaires are ahead of the game; they hardly ever think in the past or present. Their entire lives are lived in the future.

The rest of the world may perceive millionaires' positive energy and confidence as arrogance. Well, if you want what they have, *do what they do.* There's a fine line between arrogance and confidence. Arrogance is *thinking* you're better than others, confidence is *knowing* you're the best and no one is better than you. The only person you should be competing against is the person you were last year.

Work Like You're Broke

After mastering the art of psychology and establishing the right mindset, you now need to apply yourself to consistent action.

I studied the second wealthiest man in the world, Bill Gates. He took zero days off in his 20s.

I studied the third wealthiest man in the world, Warren

Buffet, through his documentary. He's almost 90 years old, yet he still wakes up early and drives to work like a normal employee. Learning this inspired and motivated me.

At age six, I developed an unstoppable work ethic on the sports field and later transferred that focus into the entrepreneurial world. This gave me an edge and put me ahead of the other 99 percent.

I created the tag line *Work Like You're Broke* to reinforce it doesn't matter who you are, where you're from, what your net worth is, what you've achieved, what you drive, or where you live. If you want to maintain and sustain your success, you need to consistently *Work Like You're Broke.*"

That's how I work. To date, I've never taken a day off.

The average millionaire has made a million and lost it four times. I am not willing to lose it; I'm not willing to get complacent. I suggest you stay in student mode where you're continuously learning, adapting, and innovating. The day you feel like you've arrived is the day you're on your way back to the place where you were last humble. Be humble or get humbled.

Discover your PIPH—Peak Income Producing Hours—your most productive times where you can be laser-focused and maximize every second.

Next, compile a list of your PIPAs—Peak Income Producing Activities—what you must do to generate revenue and results.

Once you've figured out your formula, it's time to put your head down and work harder than everyone. Imagine running on a treadmill. The more you turn up the speed, the more difficult it becomes to look left, right, or behind;

all you see is one foot in front of the other. If you look back, you'll trip and fall on your face. Find a speed that best works for you.

I went all-in, taking massive, immediate action, with sleepless nights and no parties unless I had a reason to celebrate, working long hours. I even sacrificed watching sports, which I love. I gave up TV and only watched games when I could afford to sit in the front row at the stadium. Millionaires align their life with their purpose and the reason for their existence.

Once you start to see success, remember that *we* make money, money does not make *us*.

Today, my life looks totally different. If I want to take a 365-day vacation to work smart on the beaches of the world, I can. Working hard will turn into working smart.

THE PHASES OF LIFE: ADVERSITY, PROSPERITY, AND A PLATEAU

We will all go through these phases in life; our path is non-negotiable and non-questionable. *How* you get through them is an art. As much as you accept and celebrate success and prosperity, you first need to learn how to appreciate and celebrate failure and adversity.

I want you to visualize yourself being tested on an equilibrium graph that represents these phases of life; 99% of people quit before they've completed the test. As a first move, you might go through either Prosperity or Adversity territory. Whichever you experience first, the opposite is guaranteed to happen next.

The great Jim Rohn says, "The same wind blows us all," which means we are *all* going to go through adversity, so get ready! The more you have, the more you have to lose, and the stronger you are mentally, the easier it will be to make a comeback. I've been through multiple challenges; I wouldn't be who I am if I hadn't been tested. Every self-made millionaire's story came before the glory.

I applaud those who go through Adversity first and still stick it out. The darkest point of the day is just before sunrise, and it's where most of you quit, throwing in the towel at 5:30 a.m., just before light. Can you imagine facing the Almighty one day as He plays a preview of what your life could have been if you hadn't quit at that moment?

The formula is always either Adversity or Prosperity, followed by the opposite of the first phase, and the third phase is always identical to the first phase. The fourth phase is a Plateau, a mixture of both Prosperity and Adversity. Imagine taking fives steps forward in life, and then five steps back. With one of my businesses, I had a plateau for two years, and it was frustrating with a lot of mental pain.

These phases will occur in all four pillars of your life: Health, Wealth, Relationships, and Spirituality, and not at the same time. While you are enjoying Prosperity in your business, you might suffer Adversity in your Health, and vice versa.

Life will continuously test you, though eventually you'll master it with the psychological rule we discussed earlier: *80% of life is psychological.*

You'll be wealthy beyond your wildest imagination if you survive these tests and make it through each phase.

Survive sounds like you survived a fight, right?

Yes, you did, but it'll never be a physical fight. Life will *always* be a mental battle.

Biography

The Millionaire $tudent has become a household name in more than 40 countries around the world. Just 25 years old, Sashin knows his mindset is his largest asset, and he shares his secrets in this chapter as well as in his standing-room-only talks.

Sashin Govender

Sashin grew up in Durban, South Africa. His parents introduced him to both chess and personal development when he was a young child, and he never looked back. A young chess wizard, he played in the South Africa national chess championship, and he credits much of his visionary abilities to his chess training, because he always knows his next moves in advance.

He became an entrepreneur in 2012 and has since tirelessly traveled the world. As an international motivational speaker, sales coach, and life coach, he speaks to tens of thousands of people at a time. He has business partners on every continent and is growing his business—and income—exponentially as he works tirelessly.

Contact information

Website: WinWithSashin.com
Facebook: Sashin Govender
Twitter: @WinWithSash
Instagram: @WinWithSashin
LinkedIn: Sashin Govender
YouTube: Sashin Govender

CHAPTER EIGHTEEN

Find Your '*Why*'

Joshua Wester

On December 7, 1993, in Neptune, New Jersey, during the blizzard of a lifetime, my journey began as God bestowed onto my mother one of the biggest blessings she has experienced in her life—me.

My birth gave my mother a new purpose in life and her life was no longer about just her. She had a new *why* and did everything in her power to make the best decisions possible to ensure I had the best opportunities.

All my life, it's been the two of us and I commend her for how strong she was as a single parent raising a young African-American son.

When I was 16 months old, layoffs were looming at my mother's place of employment, and she had to make a life-changing decision. Through prayers and faith, God told my mother to move to Texas. Having never visited Texas, and only knowing one person there whom she hadn't seen in more than 20 years, she took a leap of faith. She visited her friend, and while there, interviewed for a new position with the company she worked for in New Jersey, found a place for us to live, and secured childcare. That left only one thing on her list of immediate needs: a good church home.

Growing up, I always wanted a father in my life who I could go to, and I never really understood why I didn't have that in my life. When I visited my friends' homes, they had a daddy in their lives, and that bond seemed unbreakable. I dreamed about having a relationship just like that.

No matter what age you are, today can be the day you click *reset* and begin the journey God has planned for you.

Though my uncles were the father figures in my life, there is nothing comparable to the tough love and affection that comes from a father. That was something my mother could never provide. The conversations I had with my uncles and other male figures in my life were quite different from the talks I had with my mother. I was uncomfortable asking my mom questions about my body, or women, or sports, and I yearned for a father who'd understand my concerns.

I battled that question for years but always kept a positive spirit about it and told myself one day that dream would become a reality.

People often say *Be careful of what you wish for because it may just become true*. One evening my mom called me into the room, passed me the phone, and I heard a male a voice asking me for my mother's hand. My dream finally had come true—I would have a dad in my life! I was sure he and I would create that unbreakable bond every boy wants—something I never had with my biological father.

As a young kid, I didn't realize what was important in my life, but at that point, I started to realize that my *why* is *my mother.*

A new chapter of my life began; we packed our belongings and moved to Atlanta, Georgia, where my idea of the American dream—a nuclear family consisting of a father, mother, and son—was made complete. I was stoked and just so excited. I could barely wait to create a bond that I never had in my eleven years of living. A long-distance relationship wasn't ideal but they made it work and got married. Marriage was overwhelming, a big adjustment, and it was something new to all three of us. Despite the difficulties, we believed in due time we would get to know each other and function as a family.

The first few years were great. I learned the building blocks of transitioning from being a boy to a young man. It began with me assuming some chores around the house: cutting the grass, putting the trash out, and taking care of the dog. Those chores taught me discipline and routine. But the next three years after that took a complete 180-degree turn in the wrong direction; my life wasn't turning out to be as great as I thought it would be.

The man whom I called Dad had so much hate and anger built up inside that he started lashing out at my mother and me. There were two-hour commutes to and from work, school, and bills piling up every month that just added more stress to the mix. Life became a living hell.

As a teenager, I began to see myself as the problem. Verbal abuse accelerated; he would act maliciously toward me for no reason and would wait until my mother was out of the house to pounce on me. I held what was happening inside for a long time because I am the peacemaker in the family. I've always feared confrontation and never wanted to deal with it. What was happening after the first few years of the marriage was a real eye-opener. My mom and I were in complete shock because it seemed as though she married a stranger; the man he'd become was someone she had never known before.

It was not long before the verbal abuse evolved into physical abuse, and he began to assault my mother and police were called to the house several times. Over the next three years, my mother was on a mission to get back to Texas—the state she called home.

After five years living in Atlanta, all three of us moved back to Texas, to a small town called Murphy, and we all hoped for a fresh start. We were living in my mother's dream house, and for a while it seemed as if the marriage was rekindled and working well.

After a few months, my mom's husband reverted to his old self, and that's how I learned when somebody shows you who they really are, you should believe them the first time.

Fear is a made-up illusion in your head that feeds off your emotions

One day, I returned from a phenomenal vacation with my aunt, uncle, and two cousins. We were en route to my house, and when we arrived, I was nervous about going inside. I told them I didn't want to go in the house because my stepfather would be mad at me. I was sure he would be furious because he had called me during the vacation but I never returned his call. It was not intentional—I was an innocent kid on vacation living my best life. I walked into the house and went into his office. The first thing that came out of his mouth was, *Why in the hell did you not call me back the other day?*

At that moment, I wished I had stayed in the car. The one-way conversation continued, and he let me know that if I didn't answer the phone next time he called, there would be some serious consequences. Later, my mother came home and once again, the arguments developed. Things continued to get worse, and she pulled me to the side and asked, *What do you want to do? Are you ready to leave?*

I respect my mother so much for the fact that this was her dream house but her *why*—me—was more important than any materialistic thing that any human could offer her. I was very hesitant at first because all my life she'd worked her ass off to give me everything I needed. She made so many sacrifices to make sure I had opportunities, that I felt that she deserved something for once.

She was clear about her feelings. "I don't give a rip about any of this; this all can be replaced, but my job as a parent is to make sure you are happy. If you're not comfortable being here, you let me know and mom will figure out the rest," she assured me. I admitted I wasn't happy and believed it was time for them to split.

Shortly after our honest conversation, I moved out and began staying with my aunt, because my mother didn't want me around all the verbal abuse and negativity. The man my mother married left on a business trip on a Tuesday, and when he came back Thursday, we were gone. Two weeks later, my mom had him served with divorce papers. An important lesson my mother's marriage taught me was a clear vision of the type of dad that I *didn't* want to be when it was my turn to step into those shoes.

For most of my life, it seems like I've been trying to put the pieces of a puzzle together to create the ideal father, someone I could simply call *dad*.

There is an old African proverb that states it takes a village to raise a child, and I believe that is true. In my case, a village was certainly involved. Fortunately, I was able to absorb enough positive characteristics from coaches, family members, and my friends' dads, to successfully grow from a young boy and become a man. I am a firm believer that life doesn't happen *to* you; it happens *for* you. When

I look back on my life, I am grateful I learned that lesson because it has helped shape me into the man I am today.

After we decided to leave, life went back to normal, and it was just my mother and me again—just like old times. As a young kid, I didn't realize what was important in my life, but at that point, I started to realize that my *why* is *my mother*. Why do I do the things I do and achieve the goals I achieve? My *mother* is why. My mother's tenacity is phenomenal and she remains the biggest hero in my life.

If your *why* doesn't make you cry, it's not strong enough. Your *why* should be something that empowers you to get back up no matter what curveball life throws at you, no matter how many times you get knocked down. Your *why* needs to be written down and be something that's near and dear to your heart, so when tough times come along— and they are coming—your fire reignites and you never stop trying to fulfill your purpose here on earth.

I challenge you to find out what *your* why is, because once you figure out your why, *nothing* can stop you. The reason my mother is my why is because I've seen her struggle all my life yet she is one of the strongest persons I have ever met. My repayment to her is to provide her with time and the financial freedom to live a life that she can't even fathom, a life full of abundance.

I've identified those fears that have stopped me from stepping into my purpose. My fears are common fears, and you probably share some. They are fear of:
- The unknown
- What people close to me would think
- Stepping outside of my comfort zone

- What will happen when I do the unpopular thing.

Fear is a made-up illusion in your head that feeds off your emotions. During troubled periods in my life, I referred to God's word. One of my favorite scriptures is Joshua 1:9: *Be strong and courageous. Do not be afraid; do not be discouraged, for the LORD your God will be with you wherever you go* (New International Version).

The combination of finding your *why* and overcoming your fear will lead you to find your purpose here on earth.

Yes, failure is part of the growing process, but if you were not afraid of failure, what would you choose to do? I suggest you choose a big goal. Failure stops most people from moving forward but if you knew you could never fail, where would you be today?

When I was 22, I was exposed to personal development. This has changed my life, and has been a major focus for the last three years. As a kid, I used to hate reading, but for three years, reading has been my best friend.

I find it is very fulfilling to work on myself every day. Through personal development, I learned about personal affirmations; I discovered that speaking to yourself out loud is 10 times more powerful than passively hearing somebody else saying the same thing. The power of the mind is phenomenal, and what you feed your brain is a direct reflection of what you are going to attract in life.

Affirmations have allowed me to overcome my fears, because now I know where I'm headed, opposed to where I am at this moment.

The combination of finding your *why* and overcoming your fear will lead you to find your purpose here on earth. I strongly believe this. Finding your earthly purpose isn't an easy task by any means, and it's going to take some soul-searching, but I am certain we were not placed on earth accidentally.

Understanding your past has nothing to do with your future. You are in control of your own destiny, and *today is the day* you can step into your purpose. It is never too late to fulfill your purpose. No matter what age you are, today can be the day you click *reset* and begin the journey God has planned for you.

I share my story and hope it will inspire and help you to change yours. You *will* find your purpose in life. Remember to always lead with love and let God handle the rest.

Biography

Joshua Wester

Joshua Wester was born in Neptune, New Jersey and grew up in the suburbs of Plano, Texas, as an only child, raised by his single mother, Carole Wester.

In 2012, he graduated from Plano East Senior High School, having never missing a single day of school in thirteen years. Joshua earned a bachelor's degree in health and human performance, with a concentration in biomechanics and a minor in interdisciplinary studies, from Texas A&M Commerce in 2016. While at Texas A&M, he was a member of Alpha Phi Alpha Fraternity.

Joshua is a licensed claims adjuster for a major insurance company.

At 22, he started his network marketing journey; only three years later, he is a residual income earner and continues to climb the ranks.

When Joshua is not working, he and his mother travel around the world, creating a lifetime of memories.

Contact Information

Email: jwester12@gmail.com
Facebook: Josh Wester
Instagram: @jwester12
Twitter: @j_wesss

CHAPTER NINETEEN

Born to Win, Programmed to Lose

Nathan Blair

We all come into existence as completely blank slates. Everything we become, everything we believe, everything we know and understand, everything we want and desire is acquired knowledge. Yes, it is true we are born a winner; we competed against many millions of other biological organisms to be born. We won that race, now what?

Now we begin our journey.

In my own life, I was supported by one parent who was totally optimistic and believed everyone could do and read anything they wanted. Encyclopedias, medical books, handyman how-to references, deep works on history, memoirs, essays, plays, and literature were made available to me when I was very young. My total immersion in books complicated my life as I grew up. My young mind expanded so fast it was unchallenged in an academic sense. Adults who felt challenged or threatened by me often responded negatively out of fear, embarrassment, or a lack of understanding.

I often heard: *Who do you think you are? We are not going to talk about that right now. Where did you get that information? Well, that might be accurate, but we are not going to talk about it now.*

As I grew older, a series of mentors, coaches, and advisors taught me that we are *not* called to push down our gifts and keep them from the world.

I enjoyed the many times an authority figure gave me instructions or told me information, and I asked variations of that dreaded question, *Why?* What I meant was, "I'm asking you *why* to see if you really know or just reading from the book or lesson plan. Do you really know your stuff or just here filling up our time?"

Then there was my other parent, who was inflexible, rigid, unyielding, and exact. Everything had to be done just exactly right. Perfectionism is the silent killer of success. You either spend so much time getting something right that you've missed the opportunity to shine, or you procrastinate so much that you fail to complete the task at all.

Through all of that, I learned we were born to win, but based on circumstances, family, educational limitations or pressures, we become programmed to lose. I have not always resisted the lure of perfectionism; it was a virtually crippling habit I developed to make myself look good only if it could not be avoided, and as a crutch when I wanted to look good but hide in the shadows. Sometimes perfectionism even created a negative effect, in that the attention would be unavoidable because of my stellar results, and my exceptional efforts would then be expected all the time.

You can make money in business, even very good money, by being known as the best at something you do. But it often does not fit into other people's timeframes when the job is measured by the time it takes, not its perfection. A person who gets something 90 percent done, which is an acceptable industry standard, will earn far more money than a person who takes twice as long and delivers a perfect, 100 percent-finished job.

When I was in elementary school, I immersed myself in my town's bookmobile and its summer reading program. The program was fun and I was allowed to check out 15-20 books each week.

I read them all by the time the bookmobile returned the next week.

The librarian who drove the bookmobile would sometimes wonder whether I actually read the books I checked out. I would say proudly, "Ask me a question."

He would pick up a book he thought I could not possibly have read, flip through it, and ask, "What happened in this story?" I would give him a complete overview of the book, describe the main characters, and tell the story with a fervor that made it as real to him as it was to me. That exchange went on for several years and many, many summer-reader awards for the most books read during the summer.

One day, I just stopped reading all the time. Truthfully, the change was probably triggered by my parents' arguments about my constant reading. About the same time, I also learned it was much easier to hold back my knowledge so I wouldn't be recognized. Knowing all the answers generated too much attention in school. When a child holds up his hand all the time because he knows the answer, he's told he should give other children a chance to answer.

It seemed the systemic response to success was negative attention. Why would anyone want to succeed if it meant constant criticism and being shunned by the same people I wanted to befriend?

My desire to succeed, to make a difference, was still there—it was just tightly locked away and only occasionally reared its head when my need for recognition was so great it could no longer be contained. I did my best to tamp it down and keep a low profile.

As I became older, a series of mentors, coaches, and advisors taught me that we are *not* called to push down our gifts and keep them from the world. Instead, we are called to use those gifts to better ourselves, so we can help others become their best selves. Some people are equipped with everything they need but they do not become their best selves because of their fear, doubt, misbelief, unbelief, lack of motivation, or even lack of inspiration.

What motivates *you*? What drives you to want more or to succeed at all costs?

It's different for everyone. What inspires you? What is it that is so powerful it causes you to get out of your head, and out of your comfort zone? Is it a person? An idea? A belief? Maybe it's a realization that we all have a limited time on earth and you desire to live a life of significance.

Do not be distracted by negative thoughts. *What you think about, you bring about.* You can prove that theory easily. If you think you are going to miss a shot in basketball, golf, archery, or any other sport you choose, you most definitely will.

What is it you were taught? Were you taught to win? Were you taught that everyone is a winner and should feel good about themselves? Were you taught when you win, you should be gracious to those who did not win?

Mark Twain, the celebrated American author, said it best, "The two most important days in your life are the day you are born and the day you find out why."

Do you know your *why*? Why has been described as what has the capacity to hurt you. What do you love?

You are not the *you* that others think you are; you are who your creator says you are.

You were *chosen*! What does that mean? *Webster-Merriam* defines *chosen* as:

(Entry 1 of 2)

: one who is the object of choice or of divine favor : an elect person

(Entry 2 of 2)

1 : elect

2 : selected or marked for favor or special privilege, a chosen few

In the Bible, it says:

For he chose us in him before the creation of the world to be holy and blameless in his sight. In love he predestined us for adoption to sonship through Jesus Christ, in accordance with his pleasure and will.
        —**Ephesians I, 4-5,** *New International Version*

So many people walk around forgetting they were chosen for a purpose. There is so much more than just knowing your purpose. You must take action to *apply* your purpose.

Many people search for riches when instead they should be seeking wealth and success. So, how do riches, wealth, and success differ?

Anyone can be rich. *Rich* just means you have an abundance of resources to meet your needs with a little extra left over, just in case.

Wealth, true wealth, is having an abundance of both resources and time to be able to do what you want, when you want, with whomever you want, as long as you want.

Rich is a solo event; almost anyone can achieve their own goal. *Wealth* is a team sport and can only be achieved by helping others get what they want. When you help others with their desires, you will have everything you could ever want.

You *will* be tested and tried. At that moment, you have a choice.

You can choose to dwell in the past and be the person who's defined by others and their narrow view of you.

Or, you can become the person you were chosen to

be. You will run headlong toward the problems with the fervor of a person who *knows* you will succeed, and you will have the Creator on your side.

Don't let your past steal your future. Instead let your identity be tied to your heart, and what or whom you give it to.

Success does not come by desire alone. Instead, it's the goodness inside that leads a person to a path of greatness.

If success were a mathematical equation, it might look something like this.

Desire + goodness + action = success

Many people strive for achievement, and there are some who find it. Often achievement is accompanied by a flurry of people copying the same thing because someone did it first, so therefore it must be accomplishable.

A monumental accomplishment of self is a legend, that is the now and is often fleeting and forgotten.

An accomplishment of significance is one that changes many lives and continues changing lives in the future. That is an extension of your legend and that is a legacy.

Notably, one of the greatest business coaches of all time, Zig Ziglar, is the epitome of legacy. He teaches that when you are working to improve yourself and your sales ability, the improvement is often not a leap, but rather a small step. Small steps are sometimes unnoticeable, but often they have the most profound impact upon not only the people being helped but the one helping as well.

It's the little things that make the difference. For instance, if you have already sold a person on one amount but you know the value for them is in a better product, you don't have to convince them of the full price of the better product, just the difference between what they already agreed to and the amount you are helping them to achieve.

Ziglar is also known for his insight and wisdom. He shares a secret and gives us a small shift into focus with this pearl of wisdom: *If you help others get what they want, you will get everything you want.* It's the little step, the paradigm shift of the mind that causes a person to focus outwardly on others' needs, instead of inwardly toward their own needs and wants.

Since you were created, only the creator knows what you were intended for or to do. Therefore no one can define you, not even yourself, except the one who created you.

"For I know the plans I have for you," declares the Lord, "plans to prosper you and not to harm you, plans to give you hope and a future."
—Jeremiah 29:11 *New International Version*

The key points are the plans and who has them. People often get full of themselves and blast off in a direction that the creator never intended for them to go. Luckily for those who go off course, the creator has more than one plan.

Whatever holds your heart defines your life. What do you love? Who are you? Who are you really? Now for the important question. Whose are you?

My wife used to ask me that repeatedly when I would get caught up in my own problems, trying to decide what to do. At first, I didn't get it. Then over time I understood what she was asking. I am a child of God; I am the son of a King. Not just any king, but the King of Kings, He who has the cattle on a thousand hills, with way more wealth and riches than I could ever want or need. All *I* have to do is ask and receive.

Henry Ford was not the first person to invent a car. He was the first to dream he could make cars affordable for the masses. Many people quote one of his famous sayings: "The man who thinks he can and the man who thinks he can't are both right."

Being the curious, inquisitive person I am, I wondered, *What was going on when he said that?*

After much research, I discovered Henry Ford approached a well-known mechanical engineer and asked him to construct an assembly line to mass-produce his cars. The engineer informed Mr. Ford it could not be done.

Then, Mr. Ford approached a young, untested, unproven, mechanical engineer with the same request. The young engineer quickly told Mr. Ford, "Of course I can do it!"

Same opportunity, different outcome.

That research led me to formulate my own extrapolation of Mr. Ford's famous quote:

You can always do more than you THINK you can, but you can never do more than you BELIEVE you can.

Both my version and Mr. Ford's version of his original quote helped me understand that anything is possible.

So, what you are probably wondering by now is: *What does any of this have to do with me or how does any of this apply to me?*

First, if you have admitted and accepted you are a created being, then you acknowledge that you are not here by chance.

Second, you also know you are a winner, you were created for a purpose and you will find, develop, and pursue that purpose with everything in your being.

Third, you realize you are part of something much bigger than yourself and anyone else. It then becomes a responsibility to fulfill your purpose.

Finally, anyone can be ordinary, it requires you to do nothing, help no one, leave nothing behind and to touch no one.

If you are like many reading my words, you realize you have a choice but more is expected of you.

Knowing that, there is only one way for you to go, one way for you to be, and one chance for you to do your best.

My wife has driven and pushed me to become the man I was always intended to be.

Part of one's journey to success is getting on the path and never quitting until you reach the goal you were striving toward.

Persist Until Success Happens.

Biography

Nathan Blair is the winner of multiple awards in business, criminal justice, military, and academia. He was the youngest post commander for the American Legion in the State of Georgia, and was recognized as one of the top recruiters and a 100 percent goal commander—an accomplishment that had not been reached for more than a decade and hasn't been repeated.

Nathan Blair

Blair graduated from his university summa cum laude with a 4.0 grade-point average (GPA) and finished his graduate program in nine months with a 3.89 GPA.

While in the military Nathan was selected numerous times for soldier and Non-Commissioned officer of the month and quarter, receiving recognition and awards from civilian agencies, and was selected to be in a documentary about UH-60 Blackhawk helicopters. He is a veteran of the Persian Gulf War and served multiple tours overseas and stateside in Korea, Saudi Arabia, Germany, Kentucky, and New York.

After leaving the military in 1998, he entered the civilian workforce and worked in various capacities including a district manager of a national propane company, computer tech, sales and service manager for an independent computer company, and as an automobile technician for Saturn automobile company, where he received the prestigious Moment of Truth Award, which was only presented 40 times in the company's history.

While attending college, he was the recipient of a national scholarship, was published in a national criminal justice journal, won silver and gold key awards, was listed in *Who's Who in Colleges and Universities*, was on both the Dean's list and President's list, and was selected to be in a news interview and a commercial for the university.

Nathan has been in various direct sales positions or companies since 1988.

Contact Information

Email:	yourvacationplans@gmail.com
	property enterprises@gmail.com
Facebook:	Lifetime Travelers
	Nate-Blair
Instagram:	@Lifetime Travelers

CHAPTER TWENTY

Take Either Path

A.C. (Tony) Williams

When you come to a fork in the road, take either path! Make your choice and head down the path fully committed to the direction you're headed. What's important is that you do it with a positive attitude, persistent enthusiasm, and unwavering optimism, knowing you will walk the path until your success is inevitable.

The fork in the road could be a decision, a life change, even an obstacle in your current path, and could be directly or indirectly controlled by you or your actions. Realize that your persistent and God-given discipline, personal development, and perseverance can make your journey successful whichever path you take.

I have always been blessed with enthusiasm and a sense of internal optimism. In my mind, both the glass that's half-full *and* half-empty can be a positive situation. Either option gives me a shot to succeed and I simply must apply the discipline to win. I can't tell you where my belief came from, but I can show you what it is. Most importantly, I can show you how you can master it to make your chosen fork in the road a successful one.

Though I was born in "the projects," I never considered myself to have a project-to-riches success story. The public housing projects were a part of my formative life, but the so-called "project thinking" never became part of me. I see every situation as an opportunity to succeed, and the projects taught me to persevere persistently and with discipline until the situation becomes a successful story.

The one consistent theme in my life has been that I take any path of the fork in the road with enthusiasm, a positive attitude, and a strong work ethic.

Early in my life, about the time I started elementary school, my parents moved out of the inner-city projects in St. Louis, Missouri, and into a house in my beloved University City (U. City), in St. Louis County. A few years later, my parents divorced, and my mother and I moved across town with my younger brother and sister. All of these changes could have become either positive or negative experiences. Because I believed they were good changes and was determined to make sure they were, they became very positive for me.

My mother is a strong, independent woman, and she instilled the desire in my younger siblings and me to become equally strong and independent. We took on household chores, which made us well-rounded domestically, and we developed daily routines of study and play, which fostered habits leading to strong self-discipline.

Though we lived with our mother, our father was very active in our lives. While Mom created a disciplined, process-driven environment, Dad molded our mindset and encouraged us to develop an optimistic way of looking at life. One of my most memorable conversations with my father was after my Little League team lost a baseball game. Anyone who knows me also knows I take losses extremely hard; I always have. I was crying after losing the game, which was the norm for me, and I told Dad plaintively, "I never come in first at *anything*."

He smiled and I was sure something corny was coming, but instead he delivered the most profound statement I'd heard to that point, though since then I've also heard it from a host of inspirational and personal development leaders.

My father told me, "You are a winner and you will always be a winner. You want proof? I'm looking at you."

I was confused. "That doesn't make sense, Dad!"

He said, "You won the first and most important race of your life . . . you were born. Of all the sperm fighting to be the first to create life, you beat them and that is why you are here." He was right. I remember that statement triggered a hunger in me for more of that type of thinking.

Then my mother and father both remarried, and I never saw this as a problem. In my mind, we kids gained an advantage because then we had four parents instead of two.

Lastly, I realized I could outperform most of my peers academically and athletically using a strong work ethic combined with God-given talent. Looking back over those early transitions, one could see that my positive, enthusiastic mindset was developing and preparing me to deal with forks in the road.

Our family disciplines of arriving early, staying late, and "being smart" became a part of my work ethic. I always arrived early for school, athletic practices, games, meetings—*everything*—and I was always the last to leave. I always wanted more to do. I loved everything and could not get enough. Life was great in U. City. Friends, sports, and family were the best and I thrived. Simply put, this was enthusiasm personified. Even as a kid, I woke up early every day. I guess I've always wanted to get as much time out of the day as possible. These and other good habits would serve me well later in life.

The next major fork in my road was when my stepfather's job was relocated to Baton Rouge, Louisiana and we left St. Louis. I was just about to enter my freshman year of high school and was all set to enroll at U. City High with my lifelong friends. Little League and school sports such as football and baseball were the center of my life. In fact, sports would later lead me down other paths to success.

U. City had just begun football practice and planning for the new season when I learned we would move to

Baton Rouge. Even though I had no idea of what to expect with the move, I wasn't upset like most kids might have been and was truly excited and ready for new adventures. We won the city baseball championship the day before my family and I moved to Baton Rouge, and I still had no reservations about leaving. For some reason, I had an unwavering faith and was full of optimism that the future would be bright. Basically, my confidence about making any situation successful was already in place. I had reached a fork in the road and was ready to move down a different path. I had no doubt I'd succeed.

Our new situation was good. We moved from a small house in U. City to our first new middle-class home in a nice subdivision in Baton Rouge and I enrolled in a modern new high school. Tara High had carpeted areas, wood-paneled walls, newer athletic facilities, and all the amenities one could imagine.

Though I was better in baseball than football, I always had dreams of playing football for the Trojans at the University of Southern California. Well, serendipitously, my new high school colors were cardinal and gold, just like USC, and our mascot was the Trojan. What could be better?

I had no control over moving to Baton Rouge. I believed wherever we would go, I would succeed. I kept my optimism and enthusiasm and it all was turning out well and in my favor. At least I thought so.

However, a new fork in the road developed during my sophomore year. Desegregation came to Baton Rouge much later than the rest of the country and Tara High was one of the schools targeted to be desegregated. What did that mean for me? Remember our nice new subdivision home? It was in a predominantly white neighborhood, and part of the desegregation solution was to bus kids from my neighborhood to a predominantly black school in inner-city Baton Rouge. Life was throwing me a curve ball, but I didn't see it as a negative.

Because I was excelling academically and athletically at Tara High, you'd think I'd be eager to stay. However, I saw the desegregation order as just another fork in the road and a change that would be exciting. It was time to prove, once again, who I was and what I was made of. My attitude was, "Let's take this other path and make it successful."

Baton Rouge's McKinley Senior High (or McK) is a historically black high school, more than a century old, and rich in tradition and culture. McK is known for graduating Louisiana's first black high school students in 1916, and its notable alumni include Eddie G. Robinson, Lynn Whitfield, Don Cherry, H. Rap Brown, Gardener C. Taylor, and many others. As a transferring high school sophomore, none of the McK lore was known to me, and I just thought of the school as another path leading from a fork in the road. I was determined to succeed.

Ironically, about three weeks before the start of school, I learned I could have remained at Tara High School in the neighborhood where we were living because I was a minority student at a predominantly white school. The choice to stay or transfer was mine, and in my mind, either decision—to stay at Tara or leave for McKinley—would be successful. By then, though, my attitude and enthusiasm had already been refocused on succeeding at my new school, McK. I'm not sure if it was maturity or faith, but I did not hesitate to leave the modern predominantly white school with all the amenities to be bused to the inner-city, much older, predominantly black high school.

After arriving at McK, I quickly realized how blessed I was and I focused on becoming a high achiever, both academically and athletically. I collected many academic and athletic accolades at McK, culminating by being elected class president and student government president simultaneously in my senior year. I also received Most Valuable Player honors in both football and baseball and earned a baseball scholarship to Grambling State University. I had persisted until success happened.

I graduated from McK, confident in my attitude, enthusiasm, and strong work ethic, yet humble enough to know I was no better than anyone else, and ready to head down another path at Grambling State.

During my freshman year at Grambling, leaning on my disciplines aided me in my studies, with academic success being relatively easy. That gave me the luxury of spending my time and energy to prove myself on the baseball field. My enthusiasm in following what I saw as my baseball path bore fruit when I was named freshman of the year for the Southwestern Athletic Conference (SWAC). Nothing but smooth sailing from here, right?

Wrong.

Have you heard of the book, *Who Moved My Cheese?* It's all about adapting to changes and new paths, the discipline I'd been honing since I was a few years old. Well, someone moved my cheese after my freshman year at Grambling, and I was primed and ready to find new cheese. I walked into the baseball office of legendary coach Roger Cador to claim my new cheese, a baseball scholarship at Southern University. My new fork in the road led to a path through Southern University and it was time to walk it until I found success again.

In my first year at Southern University, we won the SWAC conference championship. We then went on to become the first historically black university to win a game in the NCAA Division tournament. I achieved conference recognition and was named to the All-Conference Tournament team, twice in two years from two separate universities in the same conference.

Little did I know I was to encounter another major obstacle and would face another fork in the road.

One semester I inadvertently failed to enroll in enough credit hours to maintain my eligibility, and before I realized my error, my scholarship was gone. One minute I was on top of the mountain, and the next I was at the bottom, losing it all, including my love, baseball.

Many people would have been down and maybe even out following those events. However, *I* knew whatever happened to me was not going to define me, based upon all I'd accomplished so far and where I had come from. I said, "So what! I'll have to find success another way," and set out on my new path.

There was no question whether I would stay in school, but my scholarship had vanished and I needed a job. I looked at this situation as just another fork in the road, and knew I had to choose a path and be persistent until I was successful. I consciously raised my enthusiasm level, humbled myself, and accepted a minimum-wage job washing dishes at Piccadilly Cafeterias to pay for college.

When you read this, you may think, "How can this story turn out with a good ending?" Remember my unwavering positive attitude? That combined with learning *how you do anything is how you do everything* led me to my first six-figure salary, and it all started with that dishwashing job.

Though I was doing a good job washing dishes, I was not meant to remain a dishwasher, and it showed in everything I did. An executive witnessed my work ethic, positive attitude, and level of confidence. He also knew I was still in college. He pulled me aside and showed me his payroll check.

I graduated from Southern University and moved straight down the path earning payroll checks similar to the one the executive showed me. Before I began my pursuit of success down this new path, though, I married Santa M. Warner, now my wife of almost 30 years, whom I'd also met thanks to that dishwashing job at Piccadilly.

My persistence in staying on the path to success saw us move 10 times in 10 years, from Miami, Florida, to Bakersfield, California, and many cities in between. The years right out of college were the years in which I honed my business skills. Persistence and discipline, plus developing well-rounded business skills, allowed me to flourish. First, I was looking for the big payoff like a VP or other executive title, but soon realized my success relied on sharpening my analytical and interpersonal skills, while learning to manage performance.

This readied me for the upcoming forks in the road that would firmly shape my life.

In retrospect, I had prematurely created a fork in the road when I graduated because corporate America was calling, and I enthusiastically marched down its path. My analytical skills caught the eye of recruiters, which led me down another path to a Fortune 100 company.

Climbing the corporate ladder was just another athletic game to me. I consistently and persistently applied my life disciplines, created relationships, and perfected my work ethic, while sacrificing plenty of family time. This allowed me to move quickly up a finance track. Just seven years later, my name included an executive title. Is this where my persistence to succeed would pay off?

And after 12 more years, had I truly achieved success?

My story has not ended. An entrepreneurial path outside of corporate America opened for me about five years ago. This new path allows me to combine all disciplines I learned into a concept that gives me a shot of creating a legacy for me and my family. The sacrifice of time for money required in the corporate world was no longer my definition of success, nor was owning a business that required even more of my time and truly started owning me.

I am currently PUSH-ing forward each day with a purpose in my life, while mentoring others to do the same.

Analyzing my years of corporate sacrifice and reflecting on all of the lessons I learned in high school and college, the one consistent theme has been that I take any path of the fork in the road with enthusiasm, a positive attitude, and a strong work ethic. The key is to apply them all persistently until success was in hand.

I love the fictional story about the greatest Native American rain dancer, a man who had a flawless record of making it rain no matter where he performed. During an interview years after he retired, the dancer was asked for his secret to making it rain. He answered calmly, "It rains everywhere eventually. I simply have to dance long enough until it happens."

Biography

Born and raised in St. Louis, Missouri, A.C. (Tony) Williams and his family moved to Baton Rouge, Louisiana, when he was 13. There, he attended McKinley High School, graduating with honors in academics and sports. He attended Grambling State University on a baseball scholarship, transferring to Southern University, where he graduated with a Bachelor of Science in Business. He later pursued an MBA from Louisiana State University.

A.C. (Tony) Williams

A.C. is a member of Omega Psi Phi Fraternity, Prince Hall Masons, and has served in leadership of numerous community organizations and boards.

For 20 years, A.C. successfully climbed the corporate ladder with two Fortune 100 companies, Frito Lay and RadioShack, before his desire to become an entrepreneur and mentor could no longer be contained. He currently runs a successful international direct sales business while mentoring professionals and students worldwide in entrepreneurship and personal development.

A.C. and Santa live in McKinney, Texas, near their three adult sons, Antonio Jr. (A.J.), Treyvon (T.V.), and Brandon, all of whom are in college.

Contact Information

E-mail: acwilliams.us@gmail.com
Facebook: ACWilliams
Twitter: @The_Wms_Legacy
Instagram: @the_wms_legacy

CHAPTER TWENTY-ONE

Win the Day

Philip Coldwell

Let's eliminate any future excuses right now! Let's have no more complaining, no more blaming, and no more negativity.

It all stops today.

The level of success you have attained in your life at this point is based on the decisions and habits that you have made and developed over your lifetime. The knowledge you've acquired comes from your reality. The television shows you watch, the news and the people you listen to, the music you hear, the books and publications you read, and the words you speak all influence the perspective you have on life.

When we fail, we can blame society, our environment, and the things that happen to us that are out of our control. You can complain all you want, but how well is *that* serving you? Is it taking you in the direction in which you desire to go? If not, how long do you want to continue thinking that way?

The starting point—Point A—is where you are right now. Point B is where you say you want to go in life. We must build a foundation that will keep us on the line between those two points whenever we face the inevitable obstacles that will be placed in front of us.

What you put in you is what you will become.
Spend time developing yourself and
investing in yourself.

Let's start building a foundation for future success from within ourselves by *winning the day*. Winning the day is a starting point of self-development. It's a simple, easy set of daily disciplines that focuses on eliminating negativity and creating new habits in your life. But here's the caveat—what's easy to do is even easier *not* to do.

We all develop habits that become part of our daily routines. Start now by creating good habits that take you closer to your goals. Define the goals you have set for your:

- Career
- Business
- Relationships
- Life
- Spirit

What are you interested in learning? What motivates you? What are you passionate about? Start by asking yourself very basic questions like these.

Try a little mental experiment: Start at the *end* of your life. Imagine being on your deathbed many years from now, looking back at your life. Did you pursue the ideas, the dreams, and the visions you had, or did you settle for your own excuses and complaints?

Looking at your life from different perspectives will help you define what's truly important to you. It's *your* responsibility to take ownership of your life, to serve others, and leave a legacy for future generations. Success is something you will attract by the person you become. Develop yourself, find your voice, your purpose, and your reason for being.

There are five primary components I use to *win the day.* You can use this methodology to develop any area of your life. Tailor what I do to your own goals; adjust the methodology to fit your own purpose.

I start off every day with my affirmations. (1) I affirm what I want to create, and where I'm going. *I do not want to arrive at the end of life and find myself saying "I wish I would have." When asked, I want to be able to say, "I'm glad I did."* Do affirmations two to three times a day. The words that follow "I am" follow you.

I read books (2) and listen to audios (3) for at least 15 minutes each, every day. Here's my perspective on reading books: Reading is something all successful people have in common. So, if you want to be successful, *read.* Choose books and audios about personal growth or that deal with your area of specialization.

Reach out and touch five people a day (4). The calls can be business-oriented, or a simple, *Hello, how are you.* Connect with people, as many as you can. Forming new and build existing relationships broadens your perspective.

Spend some time focusing on an income-producing activity (5). If you're in sales and marketing, it's invitations and presentations. If you're in real estate, it's showing a property or listing another. If you work for an organization, find a separate stream of income that's not related to your work environment.

Five simple steps—affirmations, reading, listening to audio, connecting, and income activity. Discipline yourself to do these five things every day, and success will happen. You're not looking for results in the beginning; instead you are breaking up your daily routine of bad habits and creating new ones.

As you prepare to step into your future armed with a new set of habits, you must implement the skills and techniques you learn.

What am I talking about?

Action.

You learn little by moving slowly and cautiously. Knowledge alone isn't enough to get you results. Action is the act of discovery. What's governing you in your life? Is it fear, doubt, belief? Your past behaviors, society, and your daily routine for years have brought you to this point. Do you fear what others will think of you? Do you believe you can actually chase your dreams down? Stop limiting yourself because of the past. There's a big difference between respecting the past and the emotional attachment that follows it.

We've led with our hearts for too long. *Follow* your heart. It's okay to have a big heart, to care, to love, to share. When you lead with your heart, it often gets broken, and that's when most people quit, give up, or succumb to the emotions that follow the heartache. Heartache doesn't feel good to anyone. Take the emotion out of the equation.

The opinions and ideas of others are just different perspectives of someone else's life. Here's the question: *Do you want the life they have?* Be careful who you listen to and what you listen to. Follow your heart but lead with your mind. It starts from developing yourself and what you put in. Win the day, day after day, and the emotional roller coaster will subside. Your emotions shift to keep you moving in a straight line toward your vision. Your belief doesn't let society, friends, or family deter you from goals. Your mind is strong and ready to take massive action.

My mentors, business coaches, and life coaches taught me how to win the day. When I ventured into my entrepreneurial life, it was my first look at personal development. My upbringing had not introduced me to any form of personal development. My life's misery factor exceeded my fear factor. I was ready to make a change, so I found an opportunity, or by the grace of God, maybe it found me. My new partnership got me excited about life again. I saw personal development and coaching for the first time on a big stage.

My first experiences gave me hope. I had no idea this type of environment existed in organizations. Over time I've discovered life isn't about me and my wants—it's about the people you serve. There's so much power in it. As you develop yourself you become more valuable in the marketplace. When I gave up the excuses, when I stopped the blaming, I focused on developing *me*. I had a direction, a sense of purpose.

For a few years, the development process went something like this: Imagine your left foot represents personal development—this new take on life, this new beginning. Your left foot stands for the skills and action required to bring your personal development to fruition. I would move my left foot, learn some skills and techniques in business, some psychology, and start building components to grow my organization, usually at an event or training. I would take my newly acquired knowledge and move my right foot, fast. I would be all action for the next few weeks, with no results. Then, I'd go back to my left foot. Maybe I had missed something in my last coaching session.

Two to three weeks would go by, and I would get ready to run again. Nothing happened. I did this repeatedly. I was spinning in circles, for long periods only moving one foot at a time. My path looked like a figure eight. I wasn't getting anywhere. I saw others around me succeeding, but not me. I felt like quitting, I felt doubtful. Should I really be pursuing this? Is it supposed to feel this way? Should I just go back to what I was good at, what everyone knows me for, where I made a living?

I had to eliminate years of bad habits, each one trying to pull me off the line. It felt like hell, I was exhausted emotionally, spiritually, and physically. Maybe it's supposed to feel this way; that's just the way it is. Maybe that's why there's so few at the top. In the bible, it says, *this too shall pass*. I read the bible daily. I am not pressing my beliefs onto you; I respect all religions and philosophies of life. Passing through is the only shortcut; know that it's temporary.

A mentor of mine showed me how to win the day: *Follow your heart, lead with your mind*. In my heart, I'm in the right place. My mind continues to grow, my emotions fuel my vision, not my results. Persistence and belief is the staircase to the top. The only way through is *through*, one step at a time, one day at a time; win the day.

Take a season of your life, a season of separation, to learn and develop the skills and habits that will propel you forward into the future. What you learn in this season, in this time frame, is more important than what you earn. What's important is what you become in the process. Your life up to this point is based on the decisions you've made and the habits you've formed. When life doesn't go your way, when life happens, how do you respond? Do you give up, do you pass blame, make excuses, or do you push through? You may have to go through hell for a little while, but you are just passing through.

Surround yourself with people who have what you want and model their success. You must do enough to get the results. How long does it take? Long enough until success happens. You keep pushing through the failure, through the doubt, through the pain, through the fear. The road you are on is supposed to feel this way. Your faith and belief must carry you until your skill can catch up.

When your new good habits start to become part of your routine, ramp up the disciplines and double the activity. Don't wait for things to be perfect. Perfection will break you. You'll spend all your time and energy thinking about how to get started and how to make everything perfect before you start. That is where fear, doubt, and disbelief win—in the mindset of perfect, in the mindset of tomorrow. Don't get done tomorrow what you can get done today. Whatever level of life you're on, you're in condition to begin. You can't gain by putting things off any longer.

Audit your thoughts daily.

Who are you listening to?

What are you listening to?

What are you speaking about?

What are you watching?

What you put in you is what you will become. Listen to audios, read books, and utilize virtual mentors, personal mentors, and coaches. Spend time developing yourself and investing in yourself. Win the day—or use another platform. Don't take your dreams, your gifts, or your talent to the grave with you.

Set yourself up to win big! Take control, stop wasting time. Nothing is going to change unless you do. You will become what you do and believe daily. Don't sabotage your own success because of the past. Cultivate a relationship with yourself; decide now. Inspiration and motivation are temporary. The beginning is where your thoughts become your reality. In the bible it says, "As you think, so you become." Do you want to grow throughout your life, or just go through life?

I spent many years serving the automotive industry. I have broad perspective in that arena. I traded time for knowledge, knowledge for income. I served the community by providing that knowledge and skill. I never asked myself how well was it serving me. What did I want to call my life's work? How can I make a global impact? What was my purpose? How do I leave a legacy for future generations?

My perception on life changed by joining an organization that fosters friendships, partnerships, and guidance. Now I'm surround by top-rank leadership, generous mentors, international speakers, global entrepreneurs, and widely recognized authorities. None of them started at the top; they all struggled when they began, and they all have pushed onward to a high level of success.

I realized I wanted to be a part of that supportive yet challenging environment. I've wasted so much time on bad habits. My habits created the life I led. Time is what it takes to create new habits. A foundation to build from is where it starts.

Win the day!

Biography

Philip Coldwell was adopted at birth and raised in Wichita, Kansas. As a life-long automotive enthusiast, he's pioneered innovations in the automotive performance industry as a business owner for 10 years (2000-2010).

He graduated from University of Phoenix with a B.A. in business while managing a branch of a Fortune 500 company in the automotive aftermarket for six years.

Philip Coldwell

His service in the automotive industry is extensive, but it's not his calling. In 2016, he partnered with a U.S.-based direct sales company. "I want to empower ridiculously good life habits and ignite real business results," he says.

Philip is building a foundation of personal growth and development and helping other do the same. *P.U.S.H.* is his first book.

Contact Information:

Email: info@philipcoldwell.com
Website: www.philipcoldwell.com
Facebook: Philip Coldwell
Instagram: @phil_of_the_future_
LinkedIn: Philip Coldwell

CHAPTER TWENTY-TWO

Choices

Conor Butts

I grew up as an only child in a house with very caring parents. My mom is a wonderful mother, even though she is disabled with primary lateral sclerosis (PLS), a rare neuromuscular wasting disease that is a non-fatal version of amyotrophic lateral sclerosis (ALS), Lou Gehrig's disease.

My mother needs a walker to get around, and for longer distances, she uses a scooter. She can't work because of her disability, and it is hard for her to maneuver in public. Unfortunately, she has also struggled with alcoholism for most of her life. She often had friends over to party, and sometimes I had to get my mom off the ground when she fell because of the dangerous combination of her disease and the alcohol. I love my mom, but I recognize she put me in so many tough situations. This made it hard for me to see life through a positive lens.

As I grew older, our family's finances got tighter. My dad taught golf, and the summer was his busy time. He spent all day, every day teaching and didn't have much time to spend with family. During the winters, he taught golf in Florida. This made it tough for me since I became the caretaker, cook, and cleaner, and had to take care of the entire household. I tell you these things to explain why sometimes I felt my life sucked. Flat out sucked.

I know now that life doesn't have to suck forever.

There were also good moments with my parents when I was growing up. My dad and I played baseball, and my mom and I always spent our free time watching different television shows together. To this day, we have not missed one season of *Big Brother*.

Freedom of choice is what allows us to decide on our goals, and from there we can take the crucial steps to reach our target.

Throughout my life there have been both good and bad circumstances. Recently, my mom developed a relationship with Jesus Christ, and as a result, she completely stopped drinking; I could not be prouder of her. My dad has always worked to make us feel comfortable, secure, and happy, and I respect him so much for what he does.

As I've matured, I've come to a major realization: If I can blame my parents for all the crappy times in my life to date, I must also blame them for all the great times that I experienced and the things I have now. I would have to blame them for the motivation that I have to succeed. So many great things have come to me through my parents, and even though I had a rough time. I can rise out of those circumstances and do more than is expected of me.

My high school years were the low point of my life and I still find them difficult to discuss. For the first time, I'll unveil my discontentment and the struggle I had finding my path. I hope sharing my story might help guide you to finding your own path.

When I became a teenager, my responsibilities at home increased and my freedom seemed to shrink to nothing. I was not happy, and I had few pleasures other than participating in a couple of sports.

I always had to get straight home to help my mom, and I took over running the household much of the year because of my dad's backbreaking schedule both in Illinois and in Florida. To escape my reality, whenever I had a chance I turned to YouTube. I found myself spending two to four hours a day aimlessly scrolling through videos, and this quickly became an unhealthy habit.

When my dad was not around, my mom and I argued far too often. She was still drinking too much and she wouldn't allow me to talk to anyone about our problems. My mom could not control much in regards of her own life, so instead, she tried to control me. I was not allowed to call my dad while he was in Florida, for she didn't want him to know about the arguments that took place while he was away. I felt trapped.

One night when my mom instructed me to pour her a vodka over ice, we began arguing over something incredibly inconsequential. Though I realized that I was upset with her because I hated when she drank and the attitude she developed that inevitably followed, I was tired of feeding her addiction. I felt I didn't have much purpose and was just living an incredibly tedious, monotonous life with no simple pleasures.

My breakthrough began when I turned a hobby into the beginning of a new life. I always loved Fantasy Football and statistics, so I got up my courage and began writing for a Fantasy Football website. I wrote weekly articles, created rankings for the upcoming year, and answered any questions the public wanted during the season. My writing replaced the wasted time I'd spent streaming YouTube for hours, and the job was a huge and positive step, the first step I made toward a potential career. I always thought I would work in sports. While I was still in high school, I also worked at an internship in sports radio and at the University of Illinois Sports Information Department. However, as life played out, my plan changed.

My dad stopped traveling to Florida each winter and stayed home with my mother so I could head off to college. I am currently enrolled at Olivet Nazarene University, where I am getting a degree in Business Administration with a focus in Management. During my freshman year, I made many friends who were all on fire for Jesus, though I didn't have a clue of the magnitude of who this Jesus character really was. I started attending church, Bible studies, and began having conversations centered around Christ. In March 2019, I finally accepted Him as my Lord and Savior.

I began by making small but positive choices to get myself out of situations that I realized might lead me down the wrong path. These choices and steps allow me to keep moving toward the life I want. I love the Oprah quote, "The biggest adventure you can take is to live the life of your dreams." The more I look at life, the more I see it as a place that needs service. From the richest to the poorest, people don't serve each other enough. I made the choice to base my life on serving. I want to serve as much as I can, Jesus was an example of a living servant, and we are called to do likewise. It is my belief that if you serve others, they will serve you back.

As I reflect on my life, I become aware of the many improvements I still need to make. Still, I have some attributes that I am proud of now. I love talking one-on-one with people because I prefer more intimate conversations and the deeper exchanges they allow. I try to learn in this way from every new person I meet.

In addition to the pleasure of learning directly from people, I just love learning in general—absorbing everything I can. Whenever I find a topic that intrigues me, I stop and take in as much new information I can find. Even the time in my life when I suffered emotionally became a blessing in disguise. The seemingly small choices we make have a snowball effect on what our lives become. My first job writing for fantasy football led me to life coaching through a flurry of small choices. As a business and life coach, I have the opportunity to help people in both personal and indirect methods, coaching them one-on-one and through the words of my books and podcasts.

If I hadn't been challenged by difficult circumstances when I was younger, I would not have the motivation I do now. I have a clear view of my future, and I owe it all to the Lord for using my circumstances to bring me where I am now. Reflect on your own life and ask yourself, *How can I use my circumstances, good and bad, to catapult my life to the next level?*

Readers, I shared this difficult part of my life story for a reason. The biggest lesson I have learned so far is that our lives are what we choose them to be. Every choice I have made has led to where I am now.

In order to receive what *you* want in life, it's crucial to understand that every choice you make is essential. The smallest steps contribute to the end goal. Choosing is your superpower now. Freedom of choice is what allows us to decide on our goals, and from there we can take the crucial steps to reach our target. Most people don't realize that the act of not making a choice is *still a choice.*

Too often I hear people say, "Bad things always happen to me."

Let me be clear. These "things that always happen to you" occur because of the choices you make. When you don't make a decision to act on an opportunity you are given, you are really saying, *This circumstance is not important to me, so I will allow others to decide the outcome for me.* You are handing over the freedom you had to decide for yourself. Don't let others make those decisions!

An example is when you want to lose weight. No one else can make you work out or eat healthier food, and *you* have to be the one to make those decisions. If you're not the one who decides, you will never be consistent enough to reach your weight-loss goal.

Many times, change is necessary, and the first place to refocus is your mindset. If you limit yourself to the capabilities you possess at any one moment, you will never believe in your true potential. As soon as you tell yourself that you won't be successful, you won't. My favorite quote from Henry Ford is a riddle: *Whether you think you can or think you can't . . . you're right.* With a handful of words, Ford clarifies the harsh truth about self-imposed limits.

One of the limiting beliefs in my own life (one with which I still struggle today) is that I tell myself I don't speak well when I'm in a group of people. I recognize this and consistently work on improving my speaking and my belief about how well I'm doing, getting into my own head to change that belief.

In the past, it was incredibly awkward whenever I met new groups of people. Since I've recognized my fear and weakness, I have been putting myself in uncomfortable group situations on purpose. I do this in order to push myself, to increase my comfort level within groups, and I know that practice will help me in the future.

Putting yourself in uncomfortable positions and pushing through limiting beliefs will help shatter your fears.

One decision I've made has impacted my life tremendously, and I want to share it with you: *Every single day I read an affirmation.* This is key to my growth and happiness, and I never skip a day. My affirmation is very simple:

I love to serve people.

At first, I believed that "serving" meant that I would acquire knowledge through helping others in different circumstances, and my thoughts focused on how *I* could benefit in the long run. Now I realize that the purpose of serving is not to benefit me in any way; it's truly just to help, assist, love, and care for others. No longer do I focus on what I can get out of the service I provide to people. Instead I focus on how I can show them the love of Jesus.

Now I look forward to serving others through life coaching as I help clients achieve their goals in personal and business life.

You've read about me and you know a little bit more about my story. Now let's focus on *you.* You are reading *PUSH* because you want to be motivated. Perhaps you're reading it to learn something from the almost two dozen great authors who have contributed their insightful and powerful chapters. It would truly be a shame if you didn't give *PUSH* another thought after you read it and just store it in your trophy bookcase to gather dust.

Instead, I challenge you to write something down about *each* chapter in *PUSH*—something you have learned or can practice to change your life for the better. Put your thoughts into writing and mark up the book; it's yours to write in, highlight, and underline.

My co-authors are inspirational, so don't waste their words. What insights do they give you? What decisions do they inspire you to make that will propel you toward a better life?

Ultimately, how can you Persist Until Success Happens into the life you want and the person you want to become? Take the time to reflect how you can make one choice right now to change your future.

Biography

Raised in Champaign, Illinois, Conor Butts is the only child of a golf coach and a disabled mother. He grew up quickly and with empathy, often taking care of his mother in the winter for months at a time while his father was coaching in Florida. His father taught him the game of golf, and he loves to play as often as he can.

Conor Butts

Though he is still a student at Olivet Nazarene University, a liberal arts college in Bourbonnais, Illinois, Conor is launching a life coaching business, and he does consultations both in person and online. He focuses on general life coaching services as well as productivity coaching for individuals and for businesses. In Conor's free time, he golfs, takes walks, and enjoys life.

Contact Information

Email: Conorbutts5@gmail.com
Phone: (217) 372-0377
Website: www.Conorbuttsss.com
Twitter: @Conorbutts5
LinkedIn: https://www.linkedin.com/in/conorbutts44/